I0409659

Desert National Wildlife Refuge Complex

Ash Meadows, Desert, Moapa Valley, and Pahranagat National Wildlife Refuges

Draft Comprehensive Conservation Plan and Environmental Impact Statement
Summary – July 2008

National Wildlife Refuge System Mission

> *To administer a national network of lands and waters for the conservation, management, and where appropriate, restoration of the fish, wildlife, and plant resources and their habitats within the United States for the benefit of present and future generations of Americans.*

Refuge Purposes

> *...for the protection, enhancement, and maintenance of wildlife resources, including bighorn sheep...* (Public Land Order 4079, dated August 31, 1966, as amended by PL 106-65).

> *...to conserve (A) fish or wildlife which are listed as endangered species or threatened species...or (B) plants...* (ESA, 16 USC Sec. 1534).

> *...suitable for (1) incidental fish and wildlife-oriented recreational development, (2) the protection of natural resources, (3) the conservation of endangered species or threatened species...* (16 USC Sec. 460k-1).

> *...the Secretary...may accept and use...real...property. Such acceptance may be accomplished under the terms and conditions of restrictive covenants imposed by donors...* (Refuge Recreation Act, as amended, 16 USC Sec. 460k-2).

> *...for use as an inviolate sanctuary, or for any other management purpose, for migratory birds...* (16 USC 715d).

U. S. Fish and Wildlife Service
California Nevada Region
2800 Cottage Way, Room W-1832
Sacramento, CA 95825

July 2008

Summary

Current Status of the Comprehensive Conservation Plan

The U.S. Fish and Wildlife Service (Service) began the process of developing a Comprehensive Conservation Plan (CCP) for the Desert National Wildlife Refuge Complex (Desert Complex) in fall 2001. Public, agency, and tribal involvement was an important part of the CCP process, with five scoping meetings held during the first year of the planning process, and multiple interagency and tribal meetings and workshops to address topics related to visitor services, cultural resources, and wildlife and habitat management. The Draft CCP/Environmental Impact Statement (EIS) is available for public review and comment starting in July 2008. The Draft CCP/EIS will be revised to respond to public comments to produce the Final CCP and Final EIS. A Record of Decision will be signed within 30 days after the availability of the Final CCP and EIS is announced in the Federal Register.

Introduction

The Desert Complex, consisting of the Ash Meadows National Wildlife Refuge (NWR), Desert NWR, Moapa Valley NWR, and Pahranagat NWR, is located in Nye, Clark, and Lincoln counties in southern Nevada (Figure 1). Ash Meadows NWR is located northwest of Pahrump, Nevada, less than 5 miles from the California-Nevada border and encompasses approximately 24,000 acres (Figure 2). Desert NWR is located less than 10 miles north of Las Vegas and encompasses more than 1.6 million acres, making it the largest refuge in the continental U.S. (Figure 3). Moapa Valley NWR is located northwest of Moapa and encompasses approximately 116 acres of land (Figure 4). Pahranagat NWR is located at the northeastern corner of the Desert NWR, just south of Alamo; this Refuge encompasses more than 5,000 acres (Figure 5). Ash Meadows and Moapa Valley NWRs were established to protect endangered and threatened species, Desert NWR was established to protect desert bighorn sheep and other wildlife, and Pahranagat NWR was established to provide a habitat for migratory birds.

Ash Meadows NWR provides habitat consisting of spring-fed wetlands and alkaline desert uplands for at least 25 plants and animals found nowhere else in the world. The Refuge has a greater concentration of endemic life than any other local area in the U.S. and the second greatest concentration in all of North America. Desert NWR provides a wide range of upland habitats, from saltbush scrub to coniferous forests, as well as natural springs and wetlands. The Refuge provides one of the largest contiguous blocks of habitat for desert bighorn sheep in the U.S. Moapa Valley NWR provides habitat for the endemic Moapa dace, including streams and springs. Pahranagat NWR provides open water, marsh, riparian, and upland habitats for migratory birds and a diversity of fish and wildlife. The Refuge is an important stopover for numerous migratory birds during their fall and spring migrations.

Comprehensive Conservation Plan Process

A CCP is prepared pursuant to the National Wildlife Refuge System Administration Act of 1966 (NWRS Administration Act), as amended by the National Wildlife Refuge System Improvement Act of 1997 (Improvement Act) (Public Law [PL] 105-57), and an EIS is prepared in accordance with the requirements of the National Environmental Policy Act of 1969 (NEPA). The Improvement Act and Part 602 (National Wildlife Refuge System Planning) of the Fish and Wildlife Service Manual provide the directives and guidance for preparing CCPs and recommends that the CCP and EIS be incorporated into one document. This approach, which provides for the direct integration of the provisions of NEPA into the CCP process, complies with the requirement that Federal agencies integrate the NEPA process with other planning at the earliest possible time.

The CCP/EIS is a programmatic document intended to analyze proposed actions on a conceptual level, except in those cases where sufficient information is available to provide project-specific analysis. Therefore, the extent of analysis provided for each restoration and/or visitor services proposal reflects the level of detail currently available for the specific proposal. The habitat restoration proposals analyzed in the CCP/EIS should be viewed as conceptual. It is during subsequent project level planning, referred to as "step-down" planning, that additional studies would be conducted, additional baseline data would be gathered, the appropriate project-level NEPA documentation would be prepared, all necessary permits would be acquired, and final engineering and restoration planning would be conducted. Step-down planning would also include a public involvement component similar to that provided during the CCP process.

The CCP is intended to provide a clear and comprehensive statement of the desired future conditions for the Refuge and to ensure public involvement in refuge management decisions. The public involvement component of CCP planning encourages public input throughout the process from initial scoping and public review of the Draft CCP to participating in refuge management decision and step-down planning following formal adoption of the plan.

Availability of the Draft CCP/EIS

The Draft CCP/EIS is available online at http://desertcomplex.fws.gov. A compact disc (CD) or hard copy of the document can be obtained by writing to: Mark Pelz, Chief, Refuge Planning, 2800 Cottage Way, W-1832, Sacramento, California 95825. Other contact methods include: 916-414-6500 (telephone), 916-414-6497 (facsimile), or fw8plancomments@fws.gov (email).

The Draft CCP/EIS is also available at the following locations: Refuge Headquarters at Ash Meadows NWR, Desert NWR, and Pahranagat NWR; Desert Complex office at 4701 N. Torrey Pines Drive; Clark County Library, 1401 E. Flamingo Road, Las Vegas, NV; Las Vegas Library, 833 Las Vegas Boulevard North, Las Vegas, NV; and North Las Vegas Library, 2300 Civic Center Drive, North Las Vegas, NV.

Purpose and Need

The purpose of developing the CCP for the refuges is to provide managers with a 15-year strategy for achieving refuge purposes and contributing to the mission of the NWRS, consistent with the sound principles of fish and wildlife conservation and legal mandates. The CCP is flexible and will be revised periodically to ensure that its goals, objectives, strategies, and timetables are valid and appropriate.

The Improvement Act requires that the Service develop a CCP for each refuge by 2012, and that refuges be managed to ensure the long-term conservation of fish, wildlife, plants, and their habitats and provides for compatible wildlife-dependent recreation. The purposes for developing a CCP are:

- To provide a clear statement of direction for the future management of the refuge;
- To provide long-term continuity in Desert Complex management;
- To communicate the Service's management priorities for the refuges to its conservation partners, neighbors, visitors, and the general public;
- To provide an opportunity for the public to help shape the future management of the refuges;
- To ensure that management programs on the refuges are consistent with the mandates of the NWR System (NWRS) and the purposes for which each refuge was established;
- To ensure that the management of the refuges fully considers resource priorities and management strategies identified in other federal, state, and local plans;
- To provide a basis for budget requests to support the refuge's needs, staffing, operations, maintenance, and capital improvements; and
- To evaluate existing and proposed uses of each refuge to ensure that they are compatible with the refuge purpose(s) as well as the maintenance of biological integrity, diversity, and environmental health.

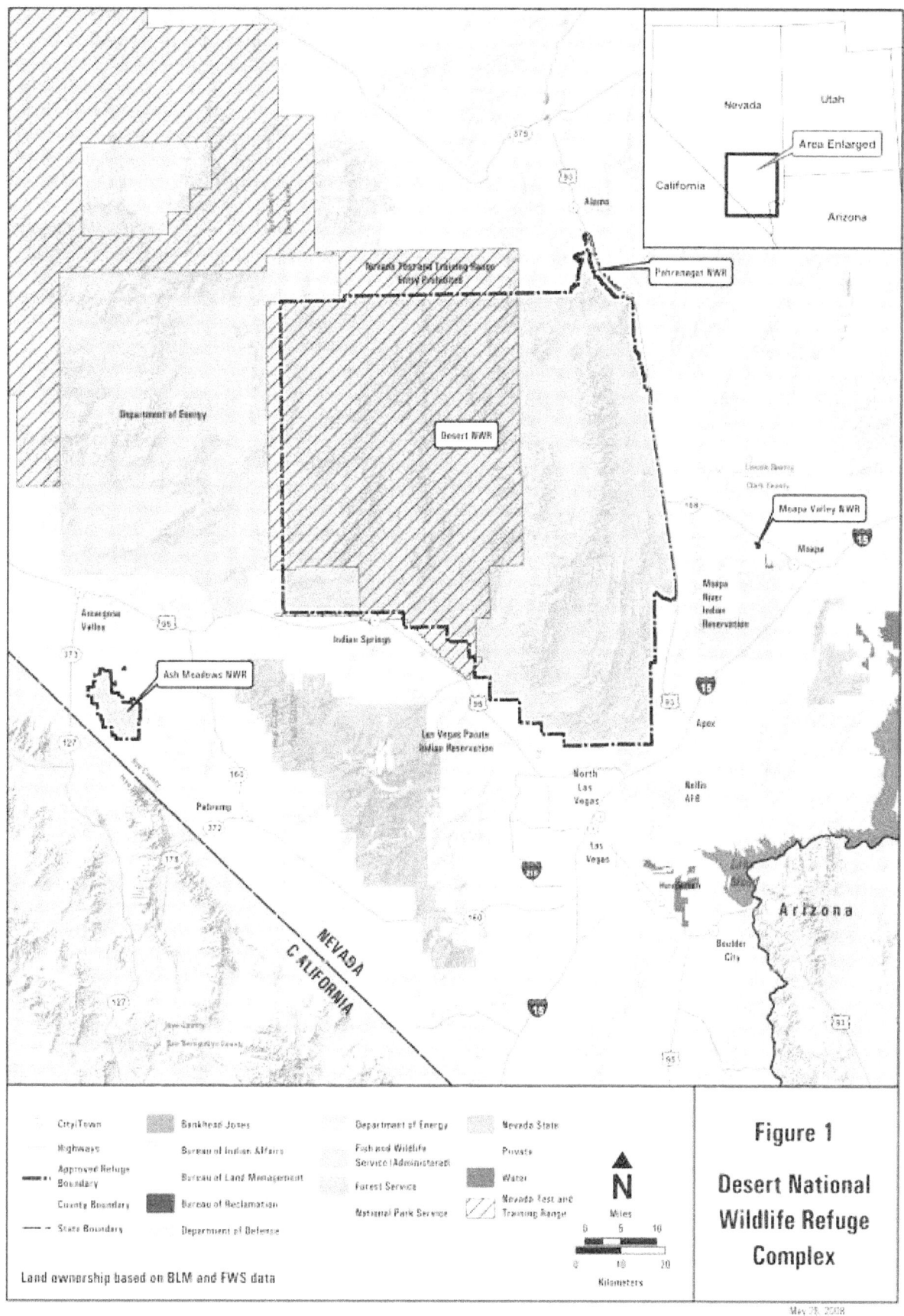

May 28, 2008
5583 130[FIGURES]40_US 20080501
Figure 1 complex land status.mxd

Figure 1

Desert National Wildlife Refuge Complex

Land ownership based on BLM and FWS data

City/Town

Highways

Approved Refuge Boundary

County Boundary

State Boundary

Bankhead-Jones

Bureau of Indian Affairs

Bureau of Land Management

Bureau of Reclamation

Department of Defense

Department of Energy

Fish and Wildlife Service (Administered)

Forest Service

National Park Service

Nevada State

Private

Water

Nevada Test and Training Range

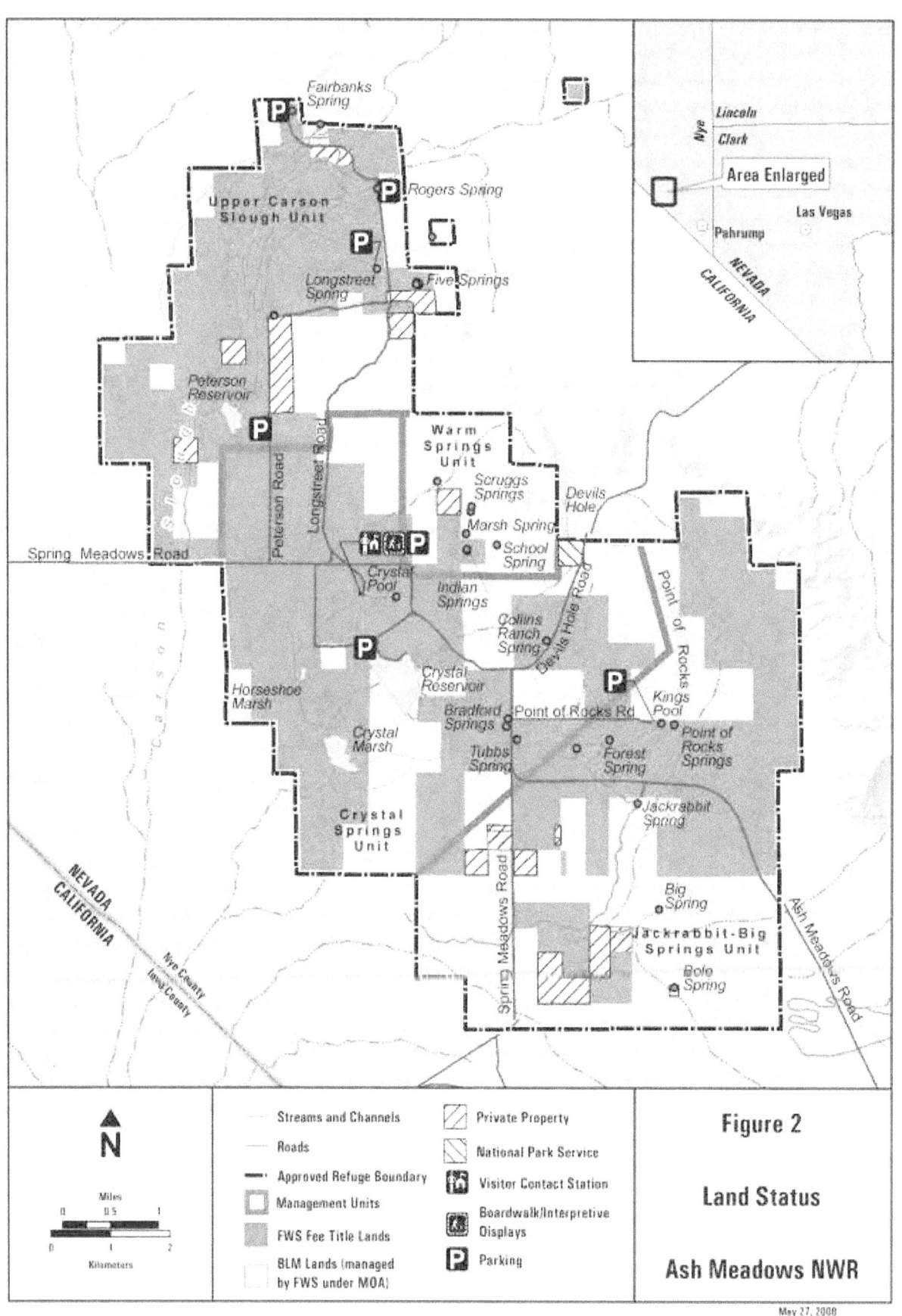

Fairbanks Spring

Upper Carson Slough Unit

Rogers Spring

Longstreet Spring

Five Springs

Peterson Reservoir

Peterson Road

Longstreet Road

Warm Springs Unit

Scruggs Springs

Devils Hole

Marsh Spring

School Spring

Spring Meadows Road

Crystal Pool

Indian Springs

Collins Ranch Spring

Devils Hole Road

Point of Rocks

Horseshoe Marsh

Crystal Reservoir

Bradford Springs

Point of Rocks Rd

Kings Pool

Crystal Marsh

Tubbs Spring

Forest Spring

Point of Rocks Springs

Crystal Springs Unit

Jackrabbit Spring

NEVADA
CALIFORNIA

Nye County
Inyo County

Spring Meadows Road

Big Spring

Jackrabbit-Big Springs Unit

Bole Spring

Ash Meadows Road

Area Enlarged

Nye | Lincoln
Clark

Las Vegas

Pahrump

NEVADA
CALIFORNIA

Figure 2

Land Status

Ash Meadows NWR

Legend	
Streams and Channels	Private Property
Roads	National Park Service
Approved Refuge Boundary	Visitor Contact Station
Management Units	Boardwalk/Interpretive Displays
FWS Fee Title Lands	Parking
BLM Lands (managed by FWS under MOA)	

N

Miles
0   0.5   1

0   1   2
Kilometers

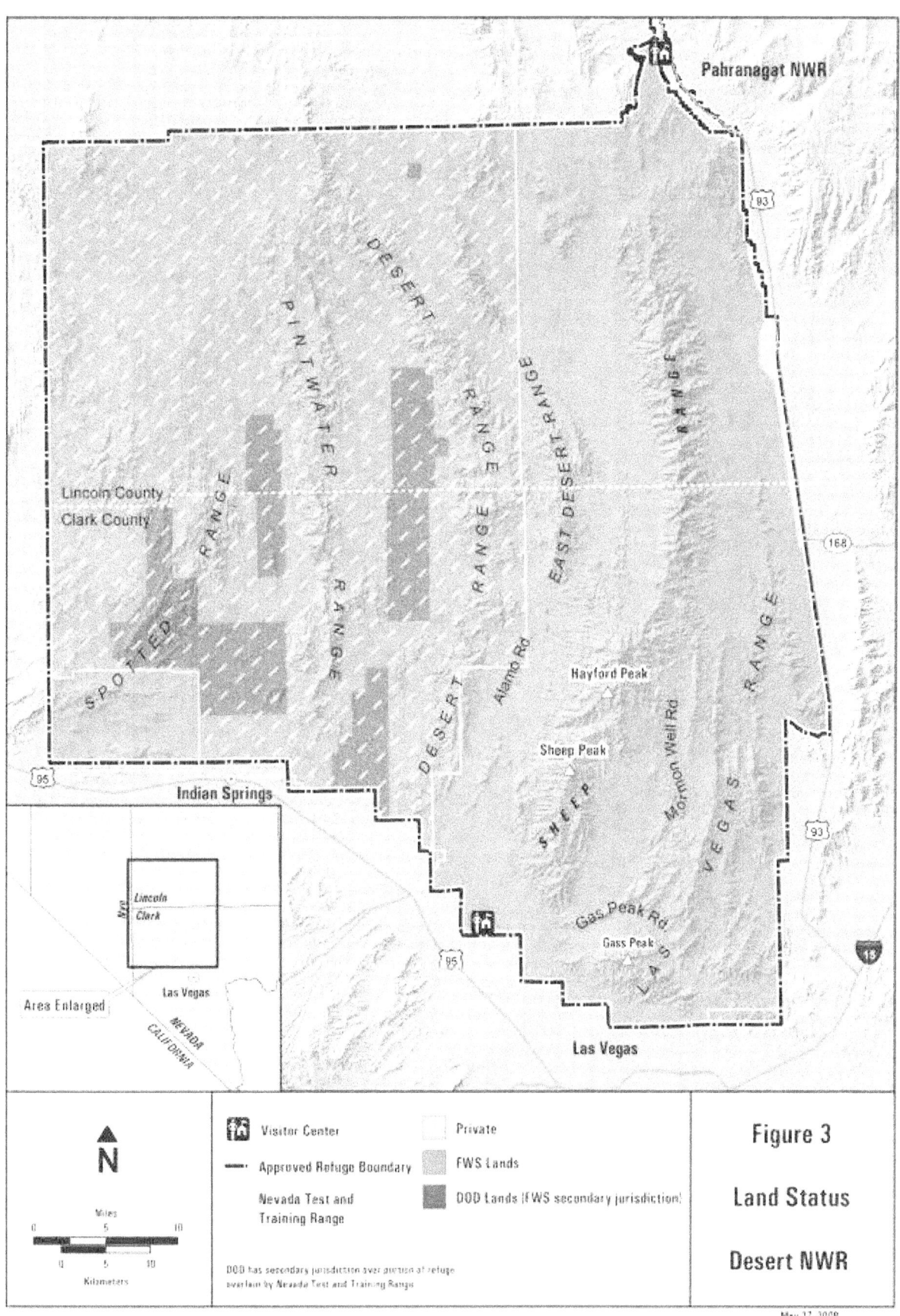

Pahranagat NWR

Lincoln County
Clark County

DESERT RANGE

PINTWATER RANGE

SPOTTED RANGE

EAST DESERT RANGE

RANGE

DESERT RANGE

Alamo Rd

Hayford Peak

Sheep Peak

Mormon Well Rd

SHEEP

VEGAS RANGE

Gas Peak Rd

Gass Peak

Indian Springs

Las Vegas

Area Enlarged

Nye
Lincoln
Clark

Las Vegas

NEVADA
CALIFORNIA

N

Miles
0   5   10

0   5   10
Kilometers

🏠 Visitor Center

— Approved Refuge Boundary

Nevada Test and
Training Range

☐ Private

FWS Lands

DOD Lands (FWS secondary jurisdiction)

DOD has secondary jurisdiction over portion of refuge
overlain by Nevada Test and Training Range

Figure 3

Land Status

Desert NWR

May 27, 2008
5683 138/FIGURESIAD EIS 20080501
Figure 3 desert landstatus.mxd

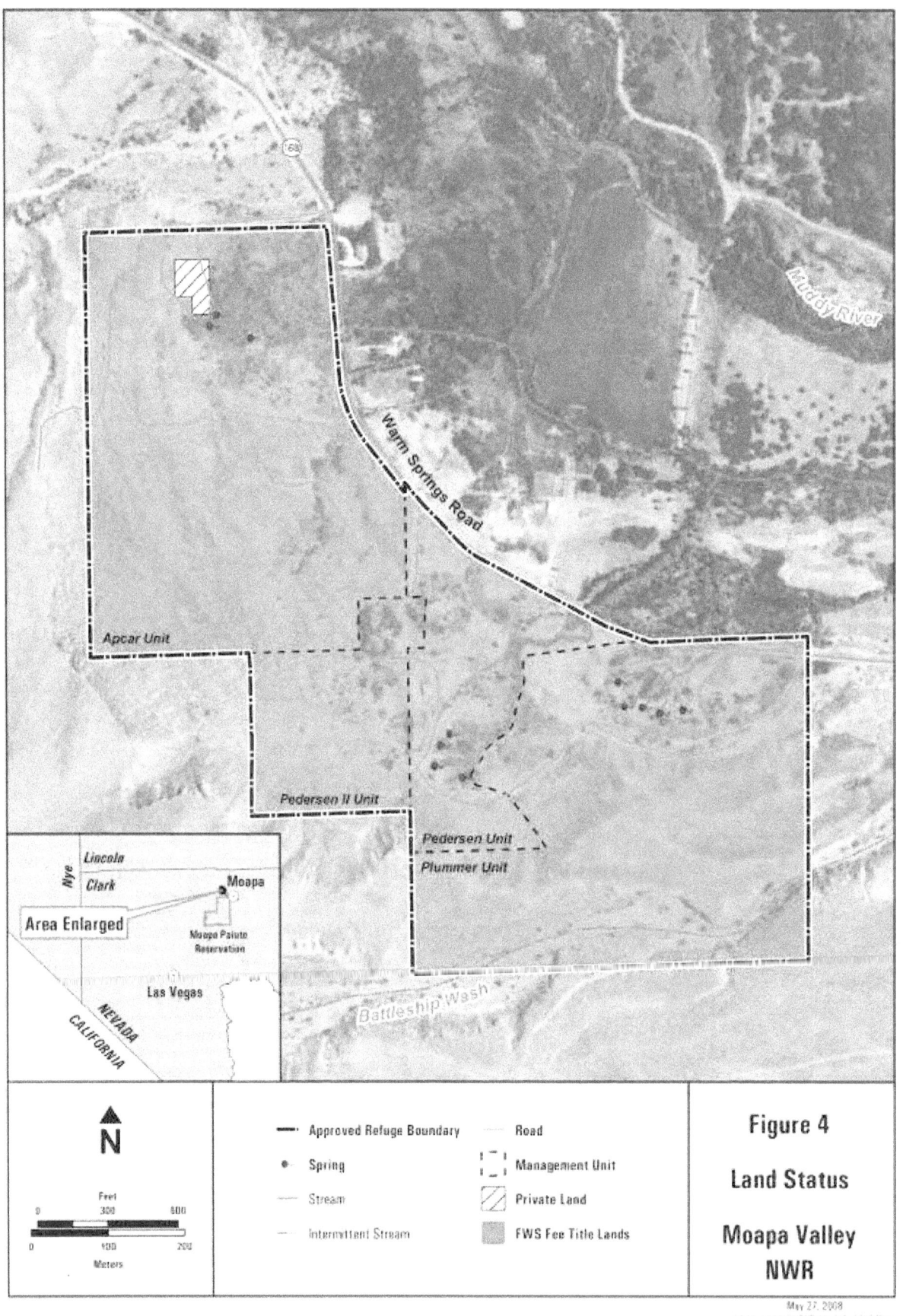

Warm Springs Road

Muddy River

Apcar Unit

Pedersen II Unit

Pedersen Unit

Plummer Unit

Battleship Wash

Nye
Lincoln
Clark
Moapa
Area Enlarged
Moapa Paiute Reservation
Las Vegas
NEVADA
CALIFORNIA

N

Feet
0   300   600

0   100   200
Meters

— Approved Refuge Boundary
● Spring
--- Stream
— Intermittent Stream

— Road
⌐ ¬
⌐ ¬ Management Unit
▨ Private Land
▨ FWS Fee Title Lands

Figure 4

Land Status

Moapa Valley NWR

May 27, 2008
5583 138/FIGURES/AO EIS 20080501
Figure 4 moapa landstatus.mxd

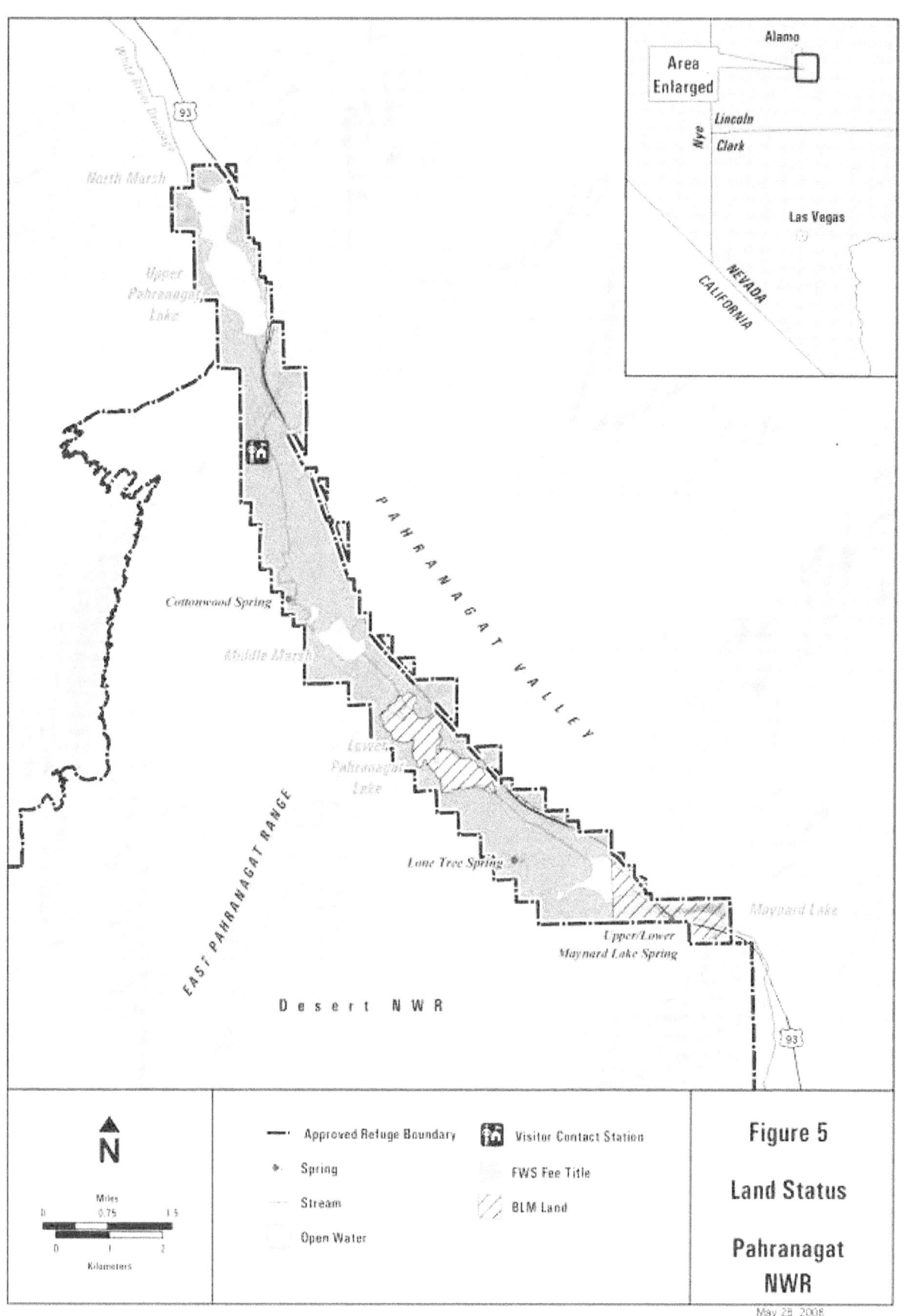

Area Enlarged

Alamo

Nye | Lincoln

Clark

Las Vegas

NEVADA

CALIFORNIA

North Marsh

Upper Pahranagat Lake

PAHRANAGAT VALLEY

Cottonwood Spring

Middle Marsh

Lower Pahranagat Lake

EAST PAHRANAGAT RANGE

Lone Tree Spring

Maynard Lake

Upper/Lower Maynard Lake Spring

Desert NWR

93

N

Miles
0   0.75   1.5

0   1   2
Kilometers

—— Approved Refuge Boundary

✦ Spring

—— Stream

Open Water

🏠 Visitor Contact Station

FWS Fee Title

BLM Land

Figure 5

Land Status

Pahranagat

NWR

May 28, 2008
5683_138\FIGURES\AD_EIS_20080501
Figure 5-pahranagat_landstatus.mxd

The National Wildlife Refuge System

The NWRS is the largest collection of lands and waters specifically managed for fish and wildlife conservation in the nation. Unlike other federal lands that are managed under a multiple use mandate (e.g., lands administered by the U.S. Bureau of Land Management and the U.S. Forest Service), the NWRS is managed for the benefit of fish, wildlife, plant resources, and their habitats.

Operated and managed by the Service, the NWRS comprises more than 545 national wildlife refuges with a combined area of more than 95 million acres. Most refuge lands (approximately 77 million acres) are in Alaska. The remaining acres are spread across the other 49 states and several island territories.

The mission of the NWRS is "*to administer a national network of lands and waters for the conservation, management and, where appropriate, restoration of fish, wildlife, and plant resources and their habitats within the United States for the benefit of present and future generations of Americans*" (16 USC 668dd et seq.).

Refuge Overview

The Desert Complex encompasses more than 1.6 million acres of land in southern Nevada in the southern part of the Great Basin and northern extent of the Mojave Desert in the Basin and Range Province. Each refuge within the Desert Complex provides important and unique habitat for wildlife, including several endemic species (species native to the refuges and often not found anywhere else). The prehistory and history of the Desert Complex region spans the last 12,000 years or more and encompasses a number of major culture areas. Visitor services vary at each refuge and are primarily focused on wildlife-dependent recreation. Each refuge also provides resources that are important to local culturally affiliated tribes.

This section provides an overview of each refuge's establishment, purpose(s), vision statement, goals, and settings.

Ash Meadows NWR

Ash Meadows NWR was established on June 18, 1984, through the purchase of 11,177 acres of former agricultural lands from The Nature Conservancy (TNC). According to the Service's 1984 Environmental Assessment: Proposed Acquisition to Establish Ash Meadows National Wildlife Refuge, the purpose of the acquisition was ". . . to protect the endemic, endangered, and rare organisms (plants and animals) found in Ash Meadows . . ." Since the original acquisition from TNC in 1984, an additional 2,309 acres have been acquired from several different landowners. Many of the Refuge's seeps, springs, pools, and streams supporting sensitive species have been destroyed or altered by human activities over the last 100 years. Habitat alterations during agricultural, municipal, and mining development caused the extinction of one fish species, at least one snail species, and possibly an endemic mammal species (Ash Meadows montane vole, *Microtus montanus nevadensis*). The Refuge provides habitat consisting of spring-fed wetlands and alkaline desert uplands for at least 25 plants and animals found nowhere else in the world. The Ash Meadows NWR has a greater concentration of endemic life than any other local area in the United States and the second greatest concentration in all of North America.

Ash Meadows NWR derives its purpose from the ESA, which authorized its creation:

> "*...to conserve (A) fish or wildlife which are listed as endangered species or threatened species...or (B) plants...*" (16 USC Sec. 1534).

The Service established the following vision statement for the Refuge during the CCP development process:

> *The springs, wetlands, and other native habitats of Ash Meadows National Wildlife Refuge support and protect the highest concentration of endemic plant and animal species anywhere in the United States. The Refuge's natural communities are restored to their historic extent and condition, and threatened and endangered species populations are recovered and maintained at sustainable levels through innovative coordination and partnerships. Refuge management continually responds to changes in the environment through adaptive management. Water supplies are ample, reliable, and of appropriate quality and temperature to sustain endemic and other fish and wildlife populations.*

> *Researchers are drawn to the Refuge where science-based management and monitoring is used to guide habitat restoration and endangered species recovery efforts and, in the process, further scientific knowledge of fields such as species genetics, regional water flow, geology and even the cultural and historical significance of this long inhabited area. Visitors find sanctuary among the crystal pools and springs nestled among the expansive Mojave Desert landscape.*

> *Local residents and visitors enjoy learning about and gaining an appreciation for the Refuge and its unique wildlife and plant species. Local educators recognize the Refuge as an exceptional regional resource for environmental education and for unique wildlife and habitat community tours. Volunteers find a meaningful and personally enriching application for their interests and talents in a responsive and appreciative setting that contributes to the conservation of rare, unique and beautiful species of wildlife and plants for the enjoyment of present and future generations of Americans.*

The following goals provide guiding principles for the Ash Meadows NWR:

Species Management (Goal 1). Restore and maintain viable populations of all endemic, endangered and threatened species within the Refuge's Mojave Desert oasis ecosystem.

Habitat (Goal 2). Restore and maintain the ecological integrity of natural communities within the Ash Meadows NWR.

Research (Goal 3). Encourage and provide opportunities for research which supports Refuge and Service objectives.

Visitor Services (Goal 4). Provide visitors with wildlife-dependent recreation, interpretation, and environmental education opportunities that are compatible with, and foster an appreciation and understanding of, Ash Meadows NWR's wildlife and plant communities.

Ash Meadows NWR is situated in the Amargosa Valley near Death Valley National Park. The Refuge provides a diversity of habitats, from springs and streams to desert uplands, and supports a variety of endemic and sensitive plant, fish, and wildlife species. Examples of species unique to the Refuge's habitats include Ash Meadows milkvetch, spring-loving centaury, Devils Hole pupfish (found only in Devils Hole, which is managed by the National Park Service), and Ash Meadows speckled dace. The Refuge also contains remnants of the past, including nearly 300 known prehistoric and/or historic sites. Several sites are eligible for listing on the National Register of Historic Places because they contain representative characteristics of the people that used the area in the past. The Refuge is a day use area, open sunrise to sunset, with numerous recreational opportunities. Wildlife-dependent activities include wildlife observation, photography, environmental education, interpretation, and hunting. Non–wildlife-dependent activities include picnicking, recreational boating, and virtual geocaching (use of geographic positioning systems for treasure hunting).

Desert NWR

On May 20, 1936, President Franklin D. Roosevelt established the Desert Game Range for "the conservation and development of natural wildlife resources" (Executive Order 7373). The 2.25 million acre Game Range, under the joint administration of the Service and Bureau of Land Management (BLM), included most of the lands within the current Refuge boundary, but stretched south to include portions of the Spring Mountains, including the area currently occupied by Red Rock Canyon National Conservation Area.

In 1939, a 320-acre ranch at Corn Creek was acquired from a private landowner under the authority of the Migratory Bird Conservation Act. This site became the administrative headquarters for the Game Range. Between 1970 and 1985, 440 acres in the vicinity of Corn Creek were purchased from a variety of private land owners under the authority of the Endangered Species Act (16 USC Sec. 1534) and Refuge Recreation Act (16 USC Sec. 460k-460).

In October of 1940, approximately 846,000 acres of the Desert Game Range were reserved for the use of the War Department (Department of Defense [DOD]) as an aerial bombing and gunnery range (now known as the Nevada Test and Training Range [NTTR]). Public Land Order 4079, dated August 31, 1966, as amended by Public Law (PL) 106-65 (Sec. 3011[b][3]), established the Desert National Wildlife Range under the sole administration of the Bureau of Sport Fisheries and Wildlife (now the Service). It also reduced the size of the refuge to 1,588,000 acres. The Military Lands Withdrawal Act of 1999 (PL 106-65) transferred primary jurisdiction of 112,000 acres of bombing impact areas on Desert NWR from the Service to the DOD. However, the Service retained secondary jurisdiction over these lands.

On November 6, 2002, President George W. Bush signed the Clark County Conservation of Public Land and Natural Resources Act of 2002 (PL 107-282), which administratively transferred 26,433 acres of BLM land adjacent to Desert NWR's east boundary to the Service. Desert NWR's land base changed again with the passage of the Lincoln County Conservation, Recreation, and Development Act of 2004 (PL 108-424). As part of the Act, administrative jurisdiction over approximately 8,382 acres of land along the eastern boundary of Desert NWR and west of U.S. Highway 93 was transferred from the Service to the BLM for use as a utility corridor. In addition, 8,503 acres of BLM-administered land were transferred to the Service to be managed as part of the Desert NWR. This land is located at the northeastern boundary of the Desert NWR and the western boundary of Pahranagat NWR.

Desert NWR is the largest Refuge in the continental United States and the largest protected area in Nevada. It encompasses six distinct mountain ranges with intervening valleys that provide a range of upland habitats for large mammals, birds, reptiles, and several sensitive species, such as the desert tortoise. Corn Creek Field Station, the Refuge headquarters, provides spring and pond habitat with wetland and riparian vegetation. The Desert NWR is one of the largest intact blocks of habitat for the bighorn sheep in the southwestern United States. The Refuge also contains two National Register Districts (Corn Creek Campsite and Sheep Mountain), which contain prehistoric and historic resources representative of past uses of the Refuge. Although only a small portion of the Refuge has been surveyed for archaeological resources, approximately 450 prehistoric sites and several historic sites have been recorded. The Refuge is also known to contain paleontological resources (fossils) dating back to the Pleistocene era (1.8 million to 10,000 years ago). The Refuge offers the opportunity for a unique and solitary desert experience. Primitive camping, picnicking, backpacking, and hiking are some of the non–wildlife-dependent recreational opportunities available on the Desert NWR. Wildlife-dependent recreational opportunities include wildlife observation, photography, and hunting.

Desert NWR has four purposes derived from laws under which it was established:

> *"...for the protection, enhancement, and maintenance of wildlife resources, including bighorn sheep..."* (Public Land Order 4079, dated August 31, 1966, *as amended by PL 106-65*).

> *"...to conserve (A) fish or wildlife which are listed as endangered species or threatened species...or (B) plants..."* (ESA, 16 USC Sec. 1534).

> *"...suitable for (1) incidental fish and wildlife-oriented recreational development, (2) the protection of natural resources, (3) the conservation of endangered species or threatened species..."* (16 USC Sec. 460k-1).

> *"...the Secretary...may accept and use...real...property. Such acceptance may be accomplished under the terms and conditions of restrictive covenants imposed by donors..."* (Refuge Recreation Act, as amended, 16 USC Sec. 460k-2).

The Service established the following vision statement for the Refuge:

> *As the largest refuge in the contiguous United States, Desert National Wildlife Range provides the highest quality, intact habitat for desert bighorn sheep and other fish, wildlife, plants and their habitats native to the Great Basin and Mojave Desert ecosystems.*

> *This rugged, arid landscape supports a full range of desert habitats from playas on the valley floors through desert scrub and coniferous woodlands to ancient bristlecone pine groves on the mountain peaks. The vast, rugged wild spaces provide wildlife and people a refuge and a place for harmonious recreational opportunities.*

The following goals provide guiding principles for the Desert NWR:

Bighorn Sheep (Goal 1). Maintain and, where necessary, restore healthy population levels of bighorn sheep on Desert NWR within each of the six major mountain ranges.

Wildlife Diversity (Goal 2). Maintain the existing natural diversity of native wildlife and plants, including special-status species, at Desert NWR.

Specially-designated Areas (Goal 3). Manage specially designated areas such that they augment the purposes of the Desert NWR.

Visitor Services (Goal 4). Visitors understand, appreciate, and enjoy the fragile Mojave/Great Basin Desert ecosystem.

Cultural Resources (Goal 5). Manage cultural resources for their educational, scientific, and traditional cultural values for the benefit of present and future generations of refuge users, communities, and culturally affiliated tribes.

Moapa Valloy NWR

Moapa Valley NWR was established on September 10, 1979, to secure and protect habitat for the endangered Moapa dace. The Refuge comprises multiple adjacent but visually distinct units. The original Pedersen Unit was acquired in 1979 and is 30 acres in size. An additional 11 acres were purchased in 2006 from Richard and Lorena Pedersen and are referred to as the Pedersen II unit. The 28-acre Plummer Unit was acquired in 1997, and the 48-acre Apcar Unit was acquired in 2000. Each unit has a separate stream system supported by the steady and uninterrupted flow of several springs that surface at various places throughout the Refuge. Due to the Refuge's small size, fragile habitats, ongoing restoration work, and removal of unsafe structures, the Refuge has been closed to the public since its establishment.

Moapa Valley NWR is situated in the Moapa Valley, east of the Desert NWR. The Refuge is part of a unique system of thermal springs that are part of the headwaters of the Muddy River, which eventually flow into Lake Mead east of Las Vegas. These springs provide riparian and aquatic habitats that support sensitive birds, bats, and fish, including the endemic Moapa dace. Most of the Refuge was previously privately held and used as a resort with swimming pools and other developed features. As a result, considerable alteration to the character of the landscape has occurred, and potential archaeological sites that may have been present are likely buried or destroyed as part of resort development. At present, due to its small size, fragile habitats, ongoing restoration work, and construction activities related to the removal of unsafe structures, the Refuge is closed to the general public. It is anticipated that the Refuge will be open to the public in the future to provide recreational opportunities once the restoration work is complete. Staff-conducted tours are currently being offered for interpretation and nature observation.

The purpose of Moapa Valley NWR derives from the ESA:

> *"...to conserve (A) fish or wildlife which are listed as endangered species or threatened species...or (B) plants..."* (16 USC Sec. 1534).

The Service established the following vision statement for the Refuge:

> *Moapa Valley National Wildlife Refuge supports and protects a healthy, thriving population of Moapa dace at the headwaters of the Muddy River. Stable flows from the Refuge's numerous warm springs fill meandering channels downstream that provide ideal habitat for dace, Virgin River chub and other species of endemic fish and invertebrates.*
>
> *The spring bank and riparian plant communities provide habitat for southwestern willow flycatcher as well as a rich diversity of migratory and resident songbirds, colonial nesting species, and other native wildlife.*
>
> *Local residents and visitors learn about and enjoy this restored desert oasis. Volunteers take personal satisfaction from contributing to the conservation and protection of Refuge wildlife and the unique spring system nourished habitats on which they depend.*

The following goals provide guiding principles for the Moapa Valley NWR:

Endemic and Special-Status Species (Goal 1). Protect and restore, when possible, healthy populations of endemic and special-status species, such as the endangered Moapa dace, within the Muddy River headwaters.

Visitor Services (Goal 2). Local communities and others enjoy and learn about the resources of Moapa Valley NWR and participate in its restoration.

Pahranagat NWR

Pahranagat NWR was established on August 16, 1963, to provide habitat for migratory birds, especially waterfowl. The Refuge is an important stopping point for numerous migratory birds during their fall and spring migrations. It is also an important tourist attraction for visitors traveling on U.S. Highway 93 to or from Las Vegas. An additional 1,466 acres were incorporated into the Refuge boundary later, bringing the acreage of Pahranagat NWR to a total of 5,382 acres.

Pahranagat NWR is situated at the southern end of Pahranagat Valley, northeast of the Desert NWR. The Refuge contains marshes, open water, native grass meadows, cultivated croplands, and riparian habitat and is an important migratory bird stopover within the Pacific flyway. The Refuge is known to support a population of federally endangered southwestern willow flycatchers and provides habitat for other sensitive birds, bats, reptiles, and mammals. The Pahranagat NWR area is an extremely important cultural landscape to many tribal people, and the Refuge contains a diversity of prehistoric and historic resources, including the Black Canyon National Register District. The public is encouraged to visit the "valley of many waters" to enjoy a variety of recreational opportunities and experience the desert oasis. Wildlife-dependent activities include wildlife observation, photography, fishing, hunting, environmental education, and interpretation. Currently, camping, boating, and picnicking are common non–wildlife-dependent activities on the Refuge.

The purpose of Pahranagat NWR derives from the Migratory Bird Conservation Act:

> *"...for use as an inviolate sanctuary, or for any*
> *other management purpose, for migratory birds..."* (16 USC 715d).

The Service established the following vision statement for the Refuge:

> *The Pahranagat National Wildlife Refuge is managed as a sanctuary where present and future generations of people can discover a connection to the rhythms of life. In spring, indigo bush and beavertail cactus bloom at the edges of verdant meadows and wetlands, fed by brimming lakes. The vital, spring-fed waters of this Mojave Desert oasis attract thousands of migratory birds each year. Pahranagat NWR's seasonal marsh, wet meadows, and alkali flats provide high quality resting and foraging habitat for wintering and migrating waterfowl, shorebirds and other waterbirds along the Pacific Flyway. Riparian gallery forests of willow, cottonwood, and associated plant communities support a flourishing population of southwestern willow flycatcher as well as a rich diversity of migratory and resident songbirds, colonial nesting species and birds of prey. Coveys of Gambel's quail emerge at dusk along with abundant cottontails and jackrabbits as nighthawks, coyotes, and owls begin to hunt. Each fall brings returning waterfowl and waterfowl hunters, while mountain lions follow mule deer down into the valley.*

> *Wetlands, wet meadows, upland plant communities, natural springs, and cultural history entice scientists and scholars to study Refuge resources and further human understanding of the processes and environments that are the foundation for the rich diversity of life on Pahranagat NWR and how humans have interacted with that environment over millennia.*

> *Other researchers focus on understanding the role of southwestern wetlands and diversity in the regional and national refuge system, the preeminent example of a habitat conservation system in the United States and perhaps the world. This ever expanding understanding contributes to conservation and management of Mojave Desert environments important to southern Nevada, the southwest, and the United States.*

> *Visitors from near and far find sanctuary among the crystal pools and springs as they learn about the Refuge's unique plant and animal communities. Local people take pride in the Refuge, and visitors tell their families and friends about this brilliant desert gem. Educators recognize the Refuge as an exceptional regional resource for environmental education and observation of wildlife and the habitats upon which they depend. Volunteers take great personal satisfaction from applying their interests and abilities to the conservation and interpretation of a unique, natural Mojave Desert community for the enjoyment of present and future generations of Americans.*

The following goals provide guiding principles for the Pahranagat NWR:

Wetland Habitat (Goal 1). Restore and maintain wetland habitat for waterfowl and other migratory birds with an emphasis on spring and fall migration feeding and resting habitat requirements.

Wildlife Diversity (Goal 2). Restore and maintain the ecological integrity of natural communities within Pahranagat NWR and contribute to the recovery of listed and other special-status species.

Visitor Services (Goal 3). Provide visitors with compatible wildlife-dependent recreation, interpretation, and environmental education opportunities that foster an appreciation and understanding of Pahranagat NWR's wildlife and plant communities.

Cultural Resources (Goal 4). Manage cultural resources for their educational, scientific, and traditional cultural values for the benefit of present and future generations of refuge users, communities, and culturally affiliated tribes.

Issues

Based on input from the public, agencies, and affiliated tribes, the following list of planning issues is a summary of the key issues that have guided the development of alternatives and preparation of the Draft CCP/EIS:

- Endemic and Federally Listed Species: How will the Service protect and restore habitat? How will the Service gather data on special-status and endemic species? What measures will the Service take to protect and restore populations of special-status species? How will the Service monitor its actions and the status of special-status species? What measures will be implemented for invasive and pest species management?
- Fires and Fuel Management: How will the Service respond to fire events or use fire to manage the refuges?
- Research: What research opportunities are available?
- Visitor Services: How will visitor service opportunities be improved or expanded? What types of opportunities will be available at each refuge? How will the Service monitor visitor use?
- Cultural Resources: How will cultural resources be managed and protected at each refuge?
- Refuge Management: What staff are needed for each refuge?
- Special Management Areas: How will special management areas (proposed wilderness, research natural areas, etc.) be managed?
- Climate Change: How will climate change affect refuge resources?

Areas of Controversy and Issues to Be Resolved

The Service has not identified any areas of controversy at this time.

The following issues will need to be resolved prior to implementation of management actions at each refuge:

- The Service's current refuge budgets and staffing would not be adequate to implement the number of new management actions that are part of the preferred alternatives. Identification of a funding source and allocation of adequate funding and staffing would be required to implement the actions.
- The Service currently lacks adequate data or information on the biological resources that occur at each refuge, specifically the extent and requirements of special-status plant and wildlife populations. Site-specific surveys of proposed restoration or affected areas would need to be conducted prior to developing restoration plans or implementing management actions to ensure the activities would benefit the species and result in minimal adverse impacts.

■ The Service currently lacks adequate data or information on the cultural resources that occur at each refuge, specifically the extent of buried or underground resources. Site-specific inventories of affected areas would need to be conducted prior to site-specific planning and implementing management actions to ensure minimal impacts on the resources.

The Service will review public comments on the Draft CCP/EIS and consider the comments during preparation of the Final CCP and Final EIS and will resolve issues raised during the comment period as appropriate.

Management Alternatives

An important step in the CCP process is the development and analysis of alternatives. Alternatives are developed to explore and analyze different ways to achieve Refuge purposes, contribute to the mission of the NWRS, meet Refuge goals, and resolve issues identified during scoping and throughout the CCP process. The alternatives developed for each Refuge are summarized below; graphics depicting the Preferred Alternatives for each refuge are included at the end of this section. Chapter 3 of the Draft CCP/EIS provides more detailed descriptions of the alternatives and graphics for each alternative.

Ash Meadows NWR

A number of current management actions would be implemented for the Ash Meadows NWR under each of the alternatives. Common to all actions include species monitoring and baseline inventories; establishment of new pupfish refugia; managing, monitoring, and restoring Refuge habitats; monitoring water resources; protecting sensitive areas of the Refuge; implementing the Integrated Pest Management Plan; completing the pending land and mineral withdrawal; acquiring private inholdings from willing sellers; and expanding visitor services and public use opportunities, specifically through construction of a boardwalk at Kings Pool and development of environmental education and interpretation materials.

Alternative A – No Action: Species management on the Refuge is currently guided by the 2006 *Geomorphic and Biological Assessment* by Otis Bay and Stevens Ecological Consulting. This document provides an overview of the resources on the Refuge and identifies recommendations for species management. Management actions identified in the document are evaluated and implemented as appropriate and as staffing and funding become available. The Service would restore 70 acres of alkali/wet meadow habitat, 30 acres of mesquite bosques/lowland riparian habitat, and 30 acres of native upland habitat in the Warm Springs and Jackrabbit/Big Springs Management Units. In addition, approximately 10 to 25 percent of the old agricultural fields would be rehabilitated by controlling invasive plants and planting native species.

The Service would continue to provide limited environmental education activities and off-Refuge outreach about the value of wildlife and the public's involvement on the Refuge. The Service would continue to inventory, manage, and protect cultural and historic resources on the Refuge on a project-by-project basis to comply with applicable laws and regulations. Appropriate educational information on cultural resources would continue to be provided to visitors at the visitor contact station through informal outreach.

Alternative B – Improve Habitat for Endemic Species on Portions of the Refuge and Increase Visitor Services: Under this alternative, the Service would improve species management on portions of the Refuge through habitat restoration and enhancement, modification of hydrology, invasive plant control, additional plant and wildlife species monitoring and research, and expanded law enforcement and protection efforts. The population of Ash Meadows speckled dace would be restored to a portion of its historic range, and the range of the Ash Meadows naucorid population would be doubled. Endemic plants would be transplanted to suitable habitat to expand their populations. Natural hydrology would be restored on portions of the Refuge, and alkali wet meadow (520 acres), mesquite bosque/lowland riparian (220 acres), emergent marsh (150 acres), and old agricultural fields (30 to 45 percent) would be restored or rehabilitated. Salt cedar and Russian knapweed would be removed and controlled to improve habitat conditions. Pest species management (e.g., crayfish) would include the 10 most infested and important Refuge aquatic systems.

Visitor services would be improved through development and implementation of Visitor Services, Outreach, and Environmental Education Plans. Educational and interpretive materials would be developed for the public. A new Refuge headquarters and visitor contact station building, as well as other visitor facilities, would be constructed, and Refuge roads would be improved to good condition. Cultural resources management would be expanded through additional inventory, monitoring, and protection efforts.

Alternative C (Preferred Alternative) – Improve Habitat for Endemic Species Throughout Refuge and Increase Visitor Services: Under this alternative, the Service would expand the management actions identified in Alternative B to improve habitat throughout the Refuge. Species inventories and monitoring would be increased, and habitat protection efforts would be expanded. The Service would expand fish populations on the Refuge to restore endemic fish populations to a portion of their historic range on the Refuge. In addition, the Service would reestablish Ash Meadows speckled dace to historic habitats after restoration of springs and streams. Natural hydrology would be restored on larger portions of the Refuge, and alkali wet meadow (650 acres), mesquite bosque/lowland riparian (550 acres), emergent marsh (150 acres), and old agricultural fields (30 to 45 percent) would be restored or rehabilitated. Pest species management would be expanded to encompass more of the Refuge and use more aggressive techniques.

Visitor services would be similar to Alternative B, except for an increase in off-site programs and a reduction in roadway and parking area improvements. An on-site research facility may be constructed. Boat use for waterfowl hunting would be restricted or eliminated.

Desert NWR

A number of current management actions would be implemented for the Desert NWR under each of the alternatives. Common to all actions include maintaining current water sources for bighorn sheep and other wildlife; continuing habitat protection measures; maintaining hunt permit limits for bighorn sheep; conducting fall surveys for bighorn sheep; prohibiting livestock grazing; managing wildfires; monitoring water resources, habitats, and wildlife; managing the Refuge to protect wilderness values; and constructing and maintaining certain visitor facilities, including a visitor center.

Alternative A – No Action: The Service would continue current bighorn sheep, wildlife, and habitat management actions that are common to all alternatives. The Air Force Overlay Area is currently managed through a Memorandum of Understanding (MOU) between the U.S. Air Force (USAF) and the Service. The current MOU would be renewed without changes. The Service would continue to provide public outreach through participation in two major community events annually. The Service would continue to manage and protect cultural resources on the Refuge on a project-by-project basis prior to land-disturbing projects to comply with applicable laws and regulations. Appropriate interpretive information on cultural resources would continue to be provided to visitors at the field station through informal outreach.

Alternative B – Minor Improvement in Wildlife and Habitat Management and Moderate Increase in Visitor Services: Under this alternative, the Service would improve bighorn sheep management and expand wildlife diversity. The Service would conduct yearly spring helicopter surveys to identify lambing and recruitment sites. Sheep would be translocated between subpopulations on the Refuge and to populations outside of the Refuge, as needed. The Service would conduct regular bird surveys at Corn Creek. Resource protection efforts would be expanded by constructing a boundary fence along the southern boundary and increase law enforcement patrols.

The MOU with the USAF would be modified to include elements for cooperative management of natural and cultural resources. Management of Research Natural Areas (RNAs) on the Refuge would be improved through boundary surveys and photographic documentation.

Visitor services would be improved through expanded environmental education and interpretive programs and an increase in visitor facilities. The Service would create a Refuge environmental education program and expand the volunteer program. Interpretation and educational efforts would be expanded through the development of new materials for the public. New visitor facilities would include wildlife viewing trails, an auto tour route, photography blinds, and parking turnouts. The Service would compile available data on cultural resources on the Refuge and expand cultural resources education and interpretive efforts.

Alternative C (Preferred Alternative) – Moderate Improvement in Wildlife and Habitat Management and Minor Increase in Visitor Services: Under this alternative, the Service would reduce some management actions compared with Alternative B, but would increase monitoring and habitat protection efforts. Bighorn sheep management would be improved through development of a Sheep Management Plan. An Inventory and Monitoring Plan would be implemented for special-status species. The Service would consider reestablishing Pahrump poolfish in the streams, ponds, or springs at Corn Creek. The Service would use prescribed burns and naturally ignited fires above 5,000 feet to restore vegetation characteristics representative of a natural fire regime. Additional resource protection measures would include fencing the eastern boundary (post and cable) where necessary, posting boundary signs along the entire southern, eastern, and northern boundaries, and expanding law enforcement presence and patrols throughout the Refuge.

The Service would submit a request to the Service Director to de-designate the Papoose Lake RNA.

Visitor services would be improved similar to Alternative B; however, an auto tour route and wildlife viewing trails would not be constructed under this alternative. The Service would distribute educational materials to the public to inform them about the use of fire for habitat management. Additional cultural resources inventories and studies would be implemented.

Alternative D – Moderate Improvement in Wildlife and Habitat Management and Limited Increase in Visitor Services: Under this alternative, the Service would implement similar wildlife management actions as Alternatives B and C with a slight increase in habitat protection. Instead of transplanting sheep between populations, as identified under Alternative B, the Service would translocate sheep from outside sources onto the Refuge as needed to maintain and increase Refuge subpopulations and improve genetic diversity. Additional habitat monitoring would occur on the Refuge. The Service would construct a post-and-cable fence along the northwest boundary of the East Pahranagat Range Unit.

Under this alternative, the Service would implement fewer management actions than Alternatives B and C with regard to visitor services. Additional visitor services related to wildlife observation and photography would be expanded as under Alternatives B; however, the Service would not improve Mormon Well and Alamo Roads, construct an auto tour route or wildlife viewing trails in Gass Peak and Sheep Range Units, or map trails at Gass Peak and Sheep Range. The volunteer program would be expanded to a lesser extent than under the other action alternatives, and public outreach and cultural resources education would be minimal.

Moapa Valley NWR

A number of current management actions would be implemented for the Moapa Valley NWR under each of the alternatives. Common to all actions include restoring habitat on the Plummer Unit, removing nonnative aquatic species from Refuge waters, surveying and monitoring Moapa dace and Moapa White River springfish populations, monitoring water resources, protecting Refuge resources, using volunteers for restoration projects, and managing cultural resources on a project-by-project basis.

Alternative A – No Action: The Service would continue current management programs with no additional habitat management. The Refuge would remain closed to the general public, and the Service would continue limited participation in local community events. Information about Refuge resources would be provided to visitors and the public upon request.

Alternative B – Improve Habitat and Wildlife Management on Portions of the Refuge and Increase Visitor Services: Under this alternative, the Service would improve habitat and wildlife management on portions of the Refuge. The alternative includes actions to restore habitat, gather baseline and population data, manage water resources, and remove invasive species. The Service would restore Moapa dace habitat on the Pedersen Unit. Inventories and monitoring would be expanded to include other endemic fish, invertebrates, and wildlife species, focusing on federally listed or other special-status species. The Service would develop a long-term Water Resources Management Plan for the Refuge and implement additional actions to improve monitoring of the springs and streams. Habitat protection efforts would also be expanded.

Visitor services would be expanded through opening of the Refuge to the public on a limited basis. New facilities would be constructed to accommodate the increase in visitors, and the environmental education and interpretation programs would be improved. The Service would develop an environmental education program and create interpretive and environmental educational materials for distribution to the public.

Alternative C (Preferred Alternative) – Improve Habitat and Wildlife Management Throughout the Refuge and Expand Visitor Services: Under this alternative, the Service would implement Refuge-wide habitat restoration efforts and expand the Refuge boundary by approximately 1,500 acres. Step-down habitat management plans would be prepared for habitats within the expanded boundary. In addition to restoring the springs and streams on the Plummer and Pedersen Units, the Service would complete restoration of the spring heads and channels on the Apcar Unit. Inventory and monitoring efforts would be expanded to include additional wildlife species.

Visitor services would be improved beyond Alternative B by opening the Refuge daily to the public and providing more programs for public use. The Service would develop an environmental education program at the Refuge and develop interpretive and environmental education materials for distribution to the public. A self-guided trail system would be constructed along the spring head, pools, and riparian corridor on the Plummer Unit to accommodate visitors. The Service would expand outreach through construction of a permanent environmental education display at the Moapa Valley Community Center or other local public venue. In addition, the Service would conduct a cultural resources inventory of the entire Refuge to assist in future planning efforts and improve management and protection of significant sites from inadvertent public visitation impacts.

Pahranagat NWR

A number of current management actions would be implemented for the Pahranagat NWR under each of the alternatives. Common to all actions include maintaining the current amounts of open water (640 acres), wet meadow (700 acres), and alkali flat (350 acres) habitats; implementing a wetland restoration plan for open water habitat; continuing water resources management to maintain the habitats; controlling carp populations; removing and controlling invasive plants; protecting Refuge habitats; implementing spring habitat Restoration Plans; monitoring Refuge habitats and plant and wildlife species; and providing a variety of recreational opportunities.

Alternative A – No Action: The Service would continue current management programs for habitat management and public use opportunities. The Service would continue to implement limited interpretation, environmental education, and outreach activities. The Service would continue to provide appropriate interpretive information on cultural resources to visitors at the visitor contact station through informal outreach and protect cultural resources on a case-by-case basis.

Alternative B – Limited Improvements in Water Resource and Habitat Management and Minor Increase in Visitor Services: Under this alternative, the Service would expand water monitoring, invasive plant removal efforts, foraging habitat for sandhill cranes, bird surveys, and habitat protection efforts. A new refugium for Pahranagat roundtail chub is also considered under this alternative pending a feasibility assessment. To increase wildlife diversity, the Service would plant and irrigate 40 acres of grain crops between Upper Pahranagat Lake and Middle Marsh.

Visitor services would be improved to accommodate an increase in visitors and monitor visitor use. The visitor contact station would be expanded to accommodate the growing number of visitors; new interpretive panels would replace old panels at the kiosk; environmental education and interpretive materials would be developed, including "least-wanted" posters for invasive plant species; and a wildlife observation trail system would be constructed throughout the Refuge, possibly along the historic farming and ranching roads. The campground would be maintained, and the Service would begin collecting fees and limit the length of stays to seven days. Cultural resources management would also be expanded to compile data on the resources at the Refuge, manage and protect the resources, and educate the public on the resources.

Alternative C – Minor Improvements in Water Resource and Habitat Management and Minor Increase in Visitor Services: Under this alternative, the Service would provide increased invasive species control, additional species inventories, additional grain crops for foraging, improved water resources management, and additional restoration of springs and riparian habitat. The Service would implement a species Inventory and Monitoring Plan for marsh birds, waterfowl, and shorebirds. To increase wildlife diversity, the Service would plant and irrigate 65 acres of grain crops. To improve habitat for the southwestern willow flycatcher, the Service would plant and establish 200 additional acres of willow habitat between Upper Pahranagat Lake and Middle Marsh.

Visitor services would also be improved similar to Alternative B, except the campground would be converted to a day use area. Visitor facilities would be improved and maintained for visitor safety, including constructing an interpretive walking trail that connects Upper Pahranagat Lake with the Headquarters Unit, constructing a new visitor contact station and office space at the Headquarters Unit, constructing additional parking at the Headquarters Unit, and constructing photography and observation blinds along the trail route. Turn lanes would be created along U.S. Highway 93 in coordination with Nevada Department of Transportation to allow visitors to safely turn onto the Refuge. Cultural resources would be inventoried, and the Service would expand cultural resources management and protection efforts.

Alternative D (Preferred Alternative) – Moderate Improvements in Water Resource and Habitat Management and Moderate Increase in Visitor Services: Under this alternative, the Service would expand upon management actions presented in Alternatives B and C, including restoring additional foraging habitat for sandhill cranes, acquiring additional water rights, expanding monitoring efforts for wildlife, and expanding invasive plant control efforts. The Service would restore the historic stream channel and riparian corridor (5–10 acres) through Black Canyon. After salt cedar is controlled around Lower Pahranagat Lake, native upland habitat would be restored. To protect the Refuge's habitats and resources and prevent encroachment, a fence would be installed along the eastern boundary.

Visitor services would be similar to Alternative B, except the campground would be converted to a day use area and vehicle access would not be allowed. In addition, the boat ramps would be closed, and a car-top boat launch would be designated. To expand cultural resources management, the Service would identify cultural resources that could educate visitors; coordinate with local affiliated tribes on their educational, scientific, and traditional cultural needs; and conduct an ethnobotany and traditional plant use study.

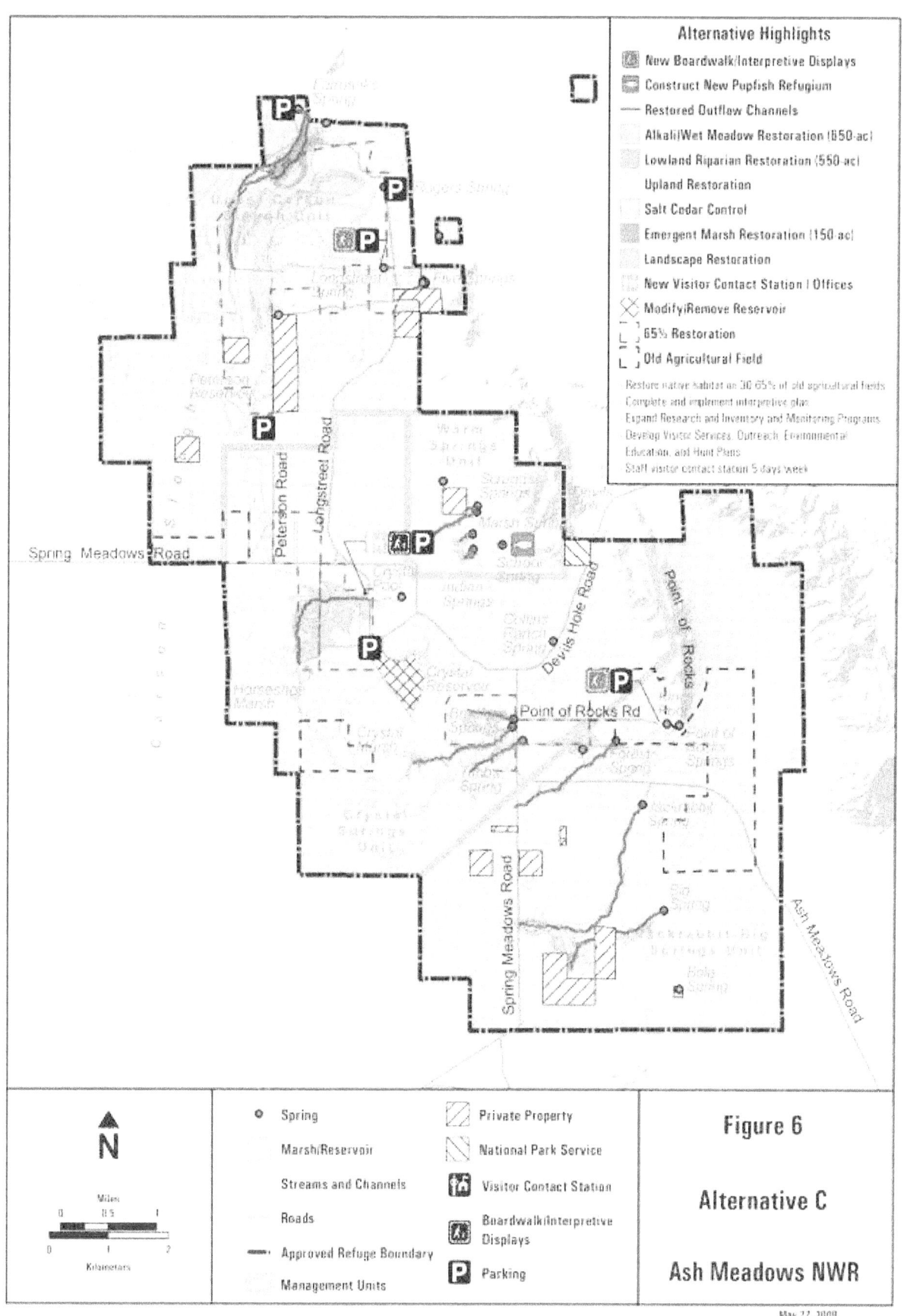

Figure 6

Alternative C

Ash Meadows NWR

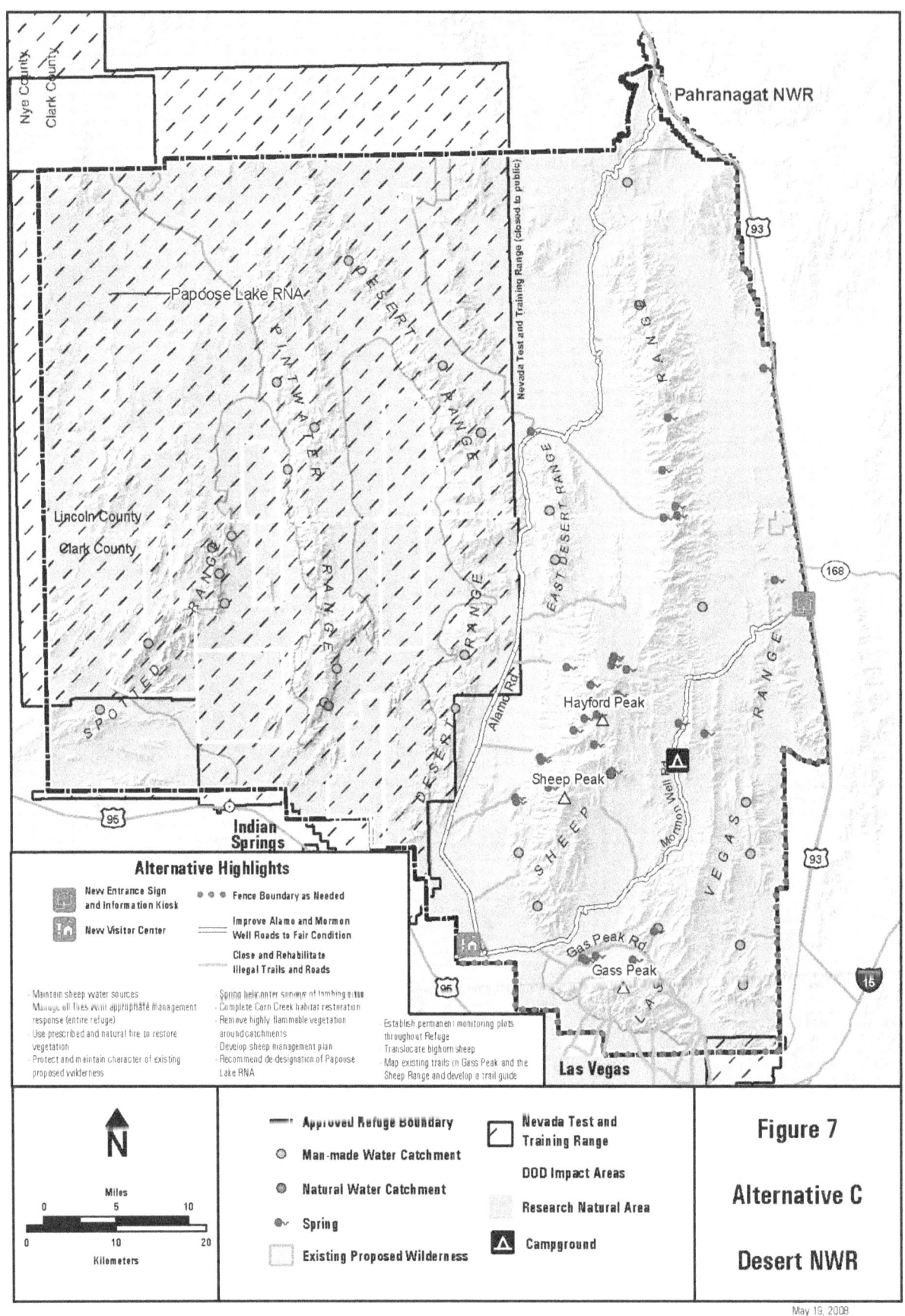

Pahranagat NWR

Papoose Lake RNA

Nye County
Clark County

Lincoln County
Clark County

Indian
Springs

Hayford Peak

Sheep Peak

Gass Peak Rd

Gass Peak

Las Vegas

Alternative Highlights

New Entrance Sign and Information Kiosk

New Visitor Center

Fence Boundary as Needed

Improve Alamo and Mormon Well Roads to Fair Condition

Close and Rehabilitate Illegal Trails and Roads

- Maintain sheep water sources
- Manage all fires with appropriate management response (entire refuge)
- Use prescribed and natural fire to restore vegetation
- Protect and maintain character of existing proposed wilderness

- Spring helicopter surveys of lambing areas
- Complete Corn Creek habitat restoration
- Remove highly flammable vegetation around catchments
- Develop sheep management plan
- Recommend de-designation of Papoose Lake RNA

- Establish permanent monitoring plots throughout Refuge
- Translocate bighorn sheep
- Map existing trails on Gass Peak and the Sheep Range and develop a trail guide

N

Miles
0   5   10

0   10   20
Kilometers

Approved Refuge Boundary

Man-made Water Catchment

Natural Water Catchment

Spring

Existing Proposed Wilderness

Nevada Test and Training Range

DOD Impact Areas

Research Natural Area

Campground

Figure 7

Alternative C

Desert NWR

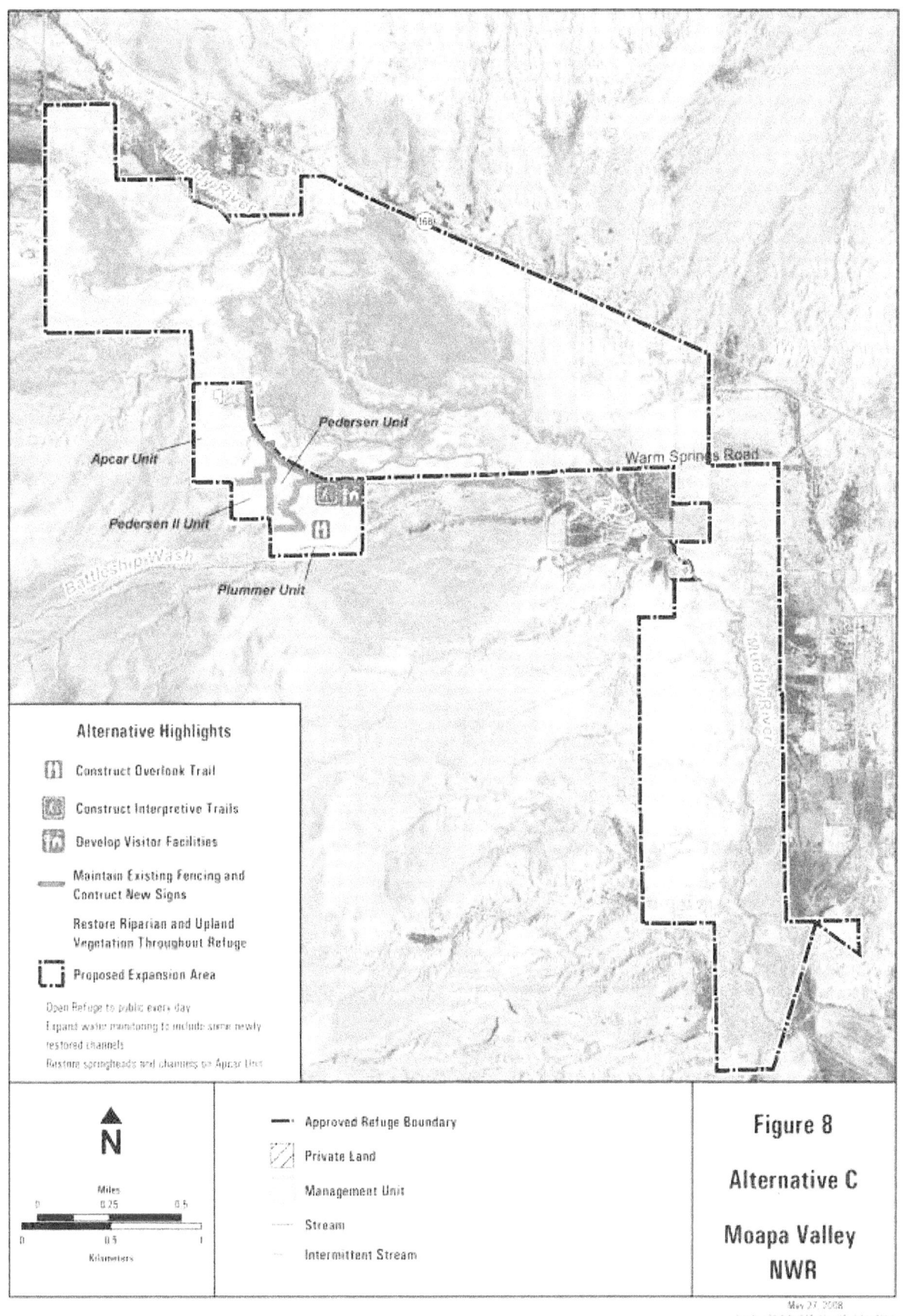

Muddy River

168

Pedersen Unit

Apcar Unit

Warm Springs Road

Pedersen II Unit

Battleship Wash

Plummer Unit

Muddy River

Alternative Highlights

⊞ Construct Overlook Trail

⊞ Construct Interpretive Trails

⊞ Develop Visitor Facilities

━━ Maintain Existing Fencing and
Construct New Signs

Restore Riparian and Upland
Vegetation Throughout Refuge

⌐ ¬ Proposed Expansion Area
└ ┘

Open Refuge to public every day
Expand water monitoring to include some newly
restored channels
Restore springheads and channels on Apcar Unit

N

Miles
0   0.25   0.5

0   0.5   1
Kilometers

━ ━ Approved Refuge Boundary

▨ Private Land

Management Unit

Stream

Intermittent Stream

Figure 8

Alternative C

Moapa Valley

NWR

May 27, 2008
5663 108/FIGURES/40_EIS 20080531
Figure 8 moapa_alt_C.mxd

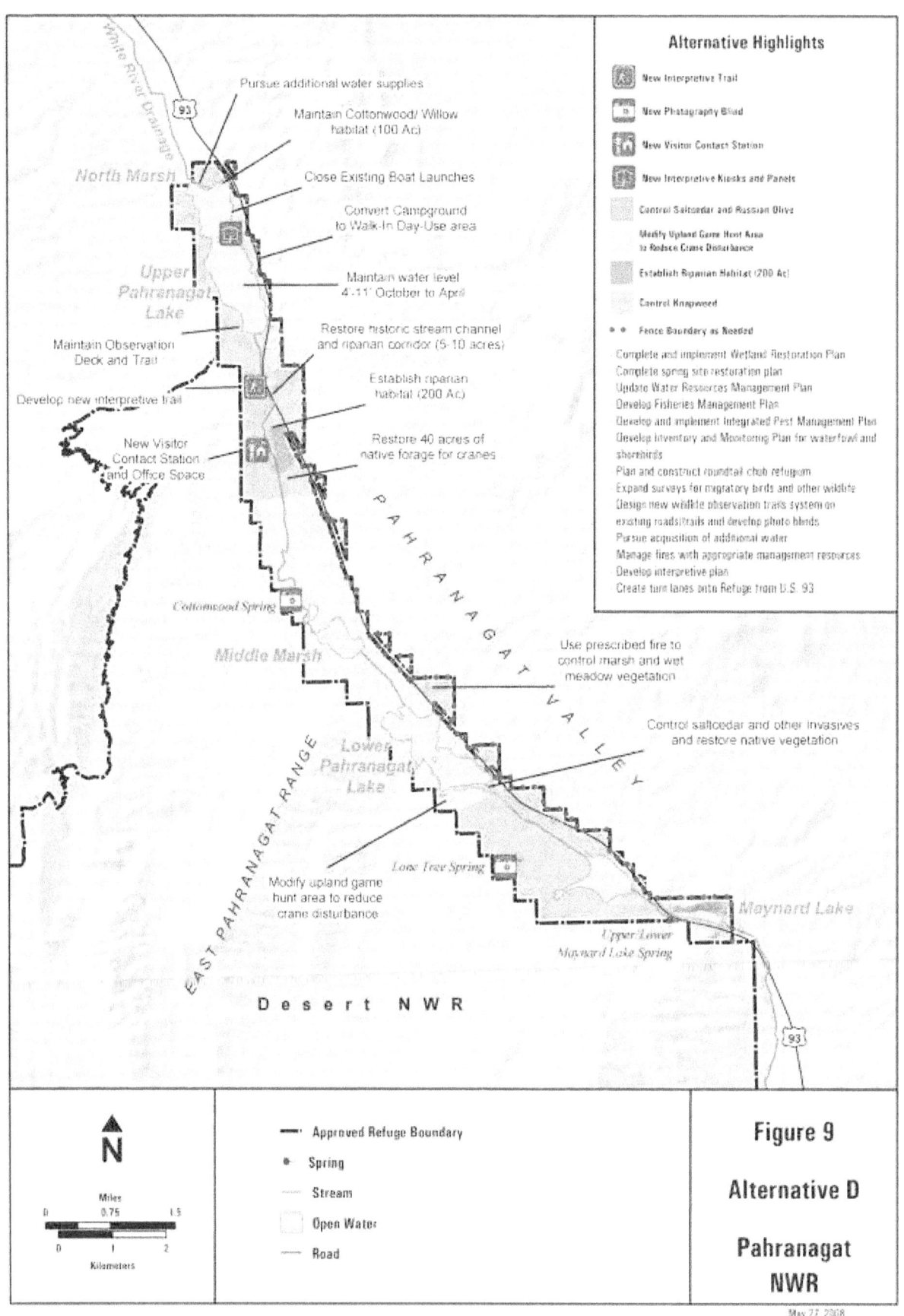

Alternative Highlights

New Interpretive Trail

New Photography Blind

New Visitor Contact Station

New Interpretive Kiosks and Panels

Control Saltcedar and Russian Olive

Modify Upland Game Hunt Area to Reduce Crane Disturbance

Establish Riparian Habitat (200 Ac)

Control Knapweed

• • Fence Boundary as Needed

Complete and implement Wetland Restoration Plan
Complete spring site restoration plan
Update Water Resources Management Plan
Develop Fisheries Management Plan
Develop and implement Integrated Pest Management Plan
Develop Inventory and Monitoring Plan for waterfowl and shorebirds
Plan and construct roundtail chub refugium
Expand surveys for migratory birds and other wildlife
Design new wildlife observation trails system on existing roads/trails and develop photo blinds
Pursue acquisition of additional water
Manage fires with appropriate management resources
Develop interpretive plan
Create turn lanes onto Refuge from U.S. 93

White River Drainage

93

North Marsh

Pursue additional water supplies

Maintain Cottonwood/ Willow habitat (100 Ac)

Close Existing Boat Launches

Convert Campground to Walk-In Day-Use area

Upper Pahranagat Lake

Maintain water level 4-11' October to April

Maintain Observation Deck and Trail

Restore historic stream channel and riparian corridor (5-10 acres)

Develop new interpretive trail

Establish riparian habitat (200 Ac)

New Visitor Contact Station and Office Space

Restore 40 acres of native forage for cranes

P A H R A N A G A T   V A L L E Y

Cottonwood Spring

Middle Marsh

Use prescribed fire to control marsh and wet meadow vegetation

Control saltcedar and other invasives and restore native vegetation

Lower Pahranagat Lake

E A S T   P A H R A N A G A T   R A N G E

Lone Tree Spring

Maynard Lake

Modify upland game hunt area to reduce crane disturbance

Upper/Lower Maynard Lake Spring

D e s e r t   N W R

93

N

Miles
0   0.75   1.5

0   1   2
Kilometers

— Approved Refuge Boundary

• Spring

— Stream

▢ Open Water

— Road

Figure 9

Alternative D

Pahranagat NWR

May 27, 2008
5583-138/FIGURES/AD_EIS_20080501
Figure 9 pahranagat_alt_D.mxd

Environmental Consequences

The Service has conducted an analysis and evaluation of the environmental consequences of implementing the various alternatives described for each refuge. This impact evaluation has considered all aspects of the affected environment, including physical, biological, cultural, and socio-economic resources. A summary of potential effects from implementing the alternatives proposed for the Ash Meadows, Desert, Moapa Valley, and Pahranagat NWRs is presented in Tables 1 through 4.

Implementation of the Proposed Action (implementing the preferred alternative for each refuge) would result in direct emission of greenhouse gases (GHG) during ground-disturbing activities (temporary emissions) due to construction and restoration projects and fire management activities (particularly fuels reduction). Fire management would help prevent catastrophic wildfire over the long term and reduce long-term GHG emissions. Indirect, long-term emissions of GHG would occur due to increased visitation by the public and increased employee vehicle trips (as staff grows).

Implementation of the preferred alternative for each refuge in combination with other reasonably foreseeable future actions in the southern Nevada region could result in cumulative impacts on physical resources (primarily water resources), biological resources (habitats and special-status species), cultural resources, and socioeconomic resources (including recreation). These impacts could be cumulatively considerable, depending on the specific nature of each action and the resources that would be affected. Larger development projects or activities that would result in a substantial amount of ground disturbance would result in cumulatively significant impacts on water quality, sensitive habitats and species, and cultural resources. Improved recreational opportunities in southern Nevada would provide a cumulative benefit to the public, and a cumulative increase in visitor use and development could improve the local economy.

Table 1.   Ash Meadows National Wildlife Refuge: Summary of Potential Effects of Implementing Alternatives A, B, or C

Resource	Alternative A	Alternative B	Alternative C (Preferred Alternative)
Physical Environment			
Soils	Temporary adverse effects related to soil erosion during restoration activities. Potential loss of topsoil from facility construction.	Same as Alternative A, only slightly more adverse. Best Management Practices (BMPs) would reduce impacts on soil.	Same as Alternative B, only more adverse.
Surface Water Hydrology	Temporary surface water diversions during refugia construction.	Same as Alternative A.	Temporary diversions during refugia construction and hydrologic restoration projects. Improved long-term surface flows from changes in hydrology.
Surface Water Quality	Potential temporary adverse effects on water quality during construction, restoration, and other ground-disturbance activities near springs, streams, and open water sources. Long-term improvement in water quality with restoration of native vegetation.	Same as Alternative A, only slightly more adverse. Greater long-term benefit from increased restoration. BMPs would reduce impacts on water quality.	Same as Alternative B, only more adverse. Greater long-term benefit from increased restoration.
Air Quality	Temporary adverse construction emissions during restoration activities and facility construction. Similar traffic-related emissions and wildfire impacts as current conditions.	Temporary adverse construction emissions during restoration activities and facility construction (slightly more adverse than Alternative A). Minor long-term increase in traffic-related emissions. Minor temporary adverse impacts from prescribed burns and wildfires. BMPs would reduce impacts on air quality.	Same as Alternative B, only more adverse.
Biological Resources			
Alkali Wet Meadow	Temporary disturbance with long-term benefit from restoration of 70 acres of alkali wet meadow.	Temporary disturbance with long-term benefit from restoration of 520 acres of alkali wet meadow.	Temporary disturbance with long-term benefit from restoration of 650 acres of alkali wet meadow.
Mesquite Bosque/Lowland Riparian	Temporary disturbance with long-term benefit from restoration of 30 acres of mesquite bosque/lowland riparian.	Temporary disturbance with long-term benefit from restoration of 220 acres of mesquite bosque/lowland riparian.	Temporary disturbance with long-term benefit from restoration of 520 acres of mesquite bosque/lowland riparian.
Emergent Marsh	Same as existing conditions.	Temporary disturbance with long-term benefit from restoration of 150 acres of emergent marsh.	Same as Alternative B.

Table 1.   Ash Meadows National Wildlife Refuge: Summary of Potential Effects of Implementing Alternatives A, B, or C

Resource	Alternative A	Alternative B	Alternative C (Preferred Alternative)
Biological Resources, continued			
Upland Habitat	Temporary disturbance with long-term benefit from restoration of 30 acres of upland habitat.	Same as Alternative A.	Same as Alternative A.
Sensitive Plants	Potential adverse impacts on sensitive plants from construction activities. Long-term benefit from habitat restoration and protection.	Greater potential for adverse impacts on sensitive plants from increased construction activities. Greater long-term benefit from increased habitat restoration and protection and transplanting. Pre-construction surveys and facility design could reduce substantial impacts to sensitive plant populations.	Same as Alternative B with a greater benefit from restoration, transplanting, and modification of Crystal Reservoir.
Invasive Plants	Long-term benefit from removal of invasive plants at restoration areas.	Greater long-term benefit from removal of invasive plants at restoration areas and controlling salt cedar and Russian knapweed populations.	Same as Alternative B with a greater benefit from salt cedar and Russian knapweed control.
Common Wildlife Species	Potential minor temporary adverse impacts from construction and restoration activities. Long-term benefit from habitat restoration and protection.	Same as Alternative A, only more adverse impacts and greater long-term benefits from habitat restoration and protection. Standard construction measures would reduce impacts during construction.	Same as Alternative B with a greater benefit from restoration.
Southwestern Willow Flycatcher	Potential temporary adverse impacts from construction and restoration activities. Minor long-term benefit from riparian habitat restoration.	Greater potential for temporary adverse impacts from increased construction and restoration activities. Greater long-term benefit from riparian habitat restoration. Pre-construction surveys and standard construction measures could reduce impacts during construction and restoration.	Same as Alternative B with a greater long-term benefit.

Table 1.   Ash Meadows National Wildlife Refuge: Summary of Potential Effects of Implementing Alternatives A, B, or C

Resource	Alternative A	Alternative B	Alternative C (Preferred Alternative)
Biological Resources continued			
Migratory Songbirds	Potential temporary adverse impacts from construction and restoration activities. Minor long-term benefit from habitat restoration.	Greater potential for temporary adverse impacts from increased construction and restoration activities. Greater long-term benefit from increased habitat restoration. Pre-construction surveys and standard construction measures could reduce impacts during construction and restoration.	Same as Alternative B with a greater long-term benefit.
Sensitive Fish	Potential temporary adverse impacts from construction and restoration activities. Improved habitat conditions with establishment of refugia and minimal control of predatory species.	Greater potential for temporary adverse impacts from increased construction and restoration activities. Greater long-term benefit from habitat restoration on portions of the Refuge, increased control of predatory and pest aquatic species, and establishment of refugia. Seasonal construction and standard construction measures, including BMPs, could reduce impacts during construction and restoration.	Same as Alternative B with a greater long-term benefit from additional restoration throughout the Refuge, including at Crystal Reservoir.
Invasive Fish	Long-term adverse impacts on sensitive fish with minimal invasive fish control efforts.	Reduced long-term adverse impacts on sensitive fish with increased invasive fish control efforts.	Greater reduction in long-term adverse impacts on sensitive fish with increased invasive fish control efforts and modification of Crystal Reservoir.
Cultural Resources			
Buried Cultural Resources	Potential adverse impacts on buried cultural resources during ground-disturbance activities.	Slightly increased potential adverse impacts on buried cultural resources during ground-disturbance activities. Mitigation measures could reduce impacts to resources during ground-disturbance.	Same as Alternative B only greater potential with more activities.
Aboveground Cultural Resources	Same as existing conditions (vandalism and degradation with minimal enforcement or protection efforts).	Reduced potential for vandalism or degradation of cultural resources from visitor use from increased law enforcement and protection efforts.	Same as Alternative B only less potential with increased law enforcement and protection.

Table 1. Ash Meadows National Wildlife Refuge: Summary of Potential Effects of Implementing Alternatives A, B, or C

Resource	Alternative A	Alternative B	Alternative C (Preferred Alternative)
Public Access and Recreation			
Public Access	Temporary access restrictions during restoration and construction activities. Long-term access same as existing (generally unrestricted).	Increase in temporary access restrictions during restoration and construction activities. Improved long-term access with road improvements and control with law enforcement and other control measures. Mitigation measures would reduce access restrictions during construction and restoration.	Same as Alternative B with greater temporary access restrictions and improved long-term access.
Recreation	Temporary restrictions on activities during restoration and construction activities. Long-term recreation opportunities same as existing.	Increase in temporary restrictions on activities during restoration and construction activities. Improved and expanded long-term recreation opportunities. Mitigation measures would reduce restrictions during construction and restoration.	Same as Alternative B with greater temporary activity restrictions and improved long-term opportunities.
Social and Economic Conditions			
Refuge Management	Same as existing conditions.	Minor increase in Refuge management budget and staff to implement the alternative.	Moderate increase in Refuge management budget and staff to implement the alternative.
Local Economics	Same as existing conditions.	Minor improvement to local economics with increase in visitors and projects.	Moderate improvement to local economics with increase in visitors and projects.
Environmental Justice	Same as existing conditions.	Minor benefit to local communities with increased recreational opportunities and improved access.	Moderate benefit to local communities with increased recreational opportunities and improved access.
Land Use	Same as existing conditions.	Reduced land use conflicts with acquisition of private parcels.	Same as Alternative B.
Aesthetics	Temporary adverse impacts during construction and restoration activities. Long-term benefits from restoration activities.	Same as Alternative A, only more temporary adverse impacts and greater long-term benefits from habitat restoration and improved facilities. Mitigation measures would reduce impacts during construction.	Same as Alternative B with a greater long-term benefit.

Table 2. Desert National Wildlife Refuge: Summary of Potential Effects of Implementing Alternatives A, B, C, or D

Resource	Alternative A	Alternative B	Alternative C (Preferred Alternative)	Alternative D
Physical Environment				
Soils	Same as existing conditions.	Potential for soil erosion from construction activities. Best Management Practices (BMPs) would reduce impacts on soil.	Potential for soil erosion from prescribed fire, but reduced potential from construction. BMPs would reduce impacts on soil.	Same as Alternative C with less erosion potential from less construction.
Surface Water Quality	Same as existing conditions.	Temporary impacts to surface water quality from construction activities. BMPs would reduce impacts on water quality.	Less adverse impacts from construction activities, and minor impacts from vegetation removal. BMPs would reduce impacts on water quality.	Same as Alternative C.
Air Quality	Same as existing conditions.	Temporary adverse construction emissions during construction activities. Minor long-term increase in traffic-related emissions. BMPs would reduce impacts on air quality.	Reduced air quality impacts from construction. Minor temporary adverse impacts from prescribed burns. Minor long-term increase in traffic-related emissions. BMPs would reduce impacts on air quality.	Same as Alternative C with reduced air quality impact from less construction.
Biological Resources				
Upland Habitat	Same as existing conditions.	Minor loss of vegetation from construction. Long-term benefit from habitat protection.	Same as Alternative B, only reduced loss of vegetation and greater long-term benefit from increased protection. Temporary disturbance from prescribed burns.	Same as Alternative C, only greater long-term benefit from increased protection.
Sensitive Plants	Same as existing conditions.	Potential for adverse impacts on sensitive plants from construction activities. Long-term benefit from increased habitat protection. Pre-construction surveys and facility design could reduce substantial impacts to sensitive plant populations.	Same as Alternative B with less potential for construction impacts and greater benefit from increased protection.	Same as Alternative C.
Common Wildlife Species	Same as existing conditions.	Potential minor temporary adverse impacts from construction activities. Standard construction measures would reduce impacts during construction.	Same as Alternative B, only less potential for construction impacts.	Same as Alternative C.

Table 2.   Desert National Wildlife Refuge: Summary of Potential Effects of Implementing Alternatives A, B, C, or D

Resource	Alternative A	Alternative B	Alternative C (Preferred Alternative)	Alternative D
Biological Resources, continued				
Desert Tortoise/Gila Monster	Same as existing conditions.	Potential temporary adverse impacts from construction activities. Minor long-term benefit from habitat protection. Pre-construction surveys and standard construction measures could reduce impacts during construction.	Same as Alternative B, only less adverse construction impacts and greater long-term benefit from increased protection.	Same as Alternative C.
Resident Birds	Same as existing conditions.	Potential temporary adverse impacts from construction activities. Minor long-term benefit from habitat protection.	Same as Alternative B, only less adverse construction impacts and greater long-term benefit from increased protection. Increased impacts from prescribed burns.	Same as Alternative C.
Bighorn Sheep	Same as existing conditions.	Temporary disturbance during construction. Long-term improvement to habitat and populations.	Same as Alternative B, only greater benefit to sheep habitat and management.	Same as Alternative C, only greater benefit to sheep management, habitat, and populations.
Sensitive Fish	Same as existing conditions.	Same as Alternative A.	Potential expanded population of Pahrump poolfish through reintroduction to Corn Creek.	Same as Alternative C.
Cultural Resources				
Buried Cultural Resources	Same as existing conditions.	Potential adverse impacts on buried cultural resources during ground-disturbance activities. Mitigation measures could reduce impacts to resources during ground disturbance.	Same as Alternative B with slightly less potential due to less ground disturbance.	Same as Alternative C.
Aboveground Cultural Resources	Same as existing conditions (vandalism and degradation with minimal enforcement or protection efforts).	Reduced potential for vandalism or degradation of cultural resources from visitor use from increased law enforcement and protection efforts.	Same as Alternative B, only less potential with increased law enforcement and protection.	Same as Alternative C, only less potential with increased protection.

Table 2.   Desert National Wildlife Refuge: Summary of Potential Effects of Implementing Alternatives A, B, C, or D

Resource	Alternative A	Alternative B	Alternative C (Preferred Alternative)	Alternative D
Public Access and Recreation				
Public Access	Same as existing conditions.	Temporary access restrictions during construction activities. Improved long-term access with road improvements and control with law enforcement and other control measures. Mitigation measures would reduce access restrictions during construction.	Same as Alternative B with greater temporary access restrictions and increased control of access.	Same as Alternative C with increased control of access.
Recreation	Same as existing conditions.	Temporary restrictions on activities during construction activities. Improved and expanded long-term recreation opportunities. Mitigation measures would reduce restrictions during construction.	Same as Alternative B with greater temporary activity restrictions and fewer long-term opportunities.	Same as Alternative C with fewer long-term opportunities.
Social and Economic Conditions				
Refuge Management	Same as existing conditions.	Minor increase in Refuge management budget and staff to implement the alternative.	Moderate increase in Refuge management budget and staff to implement the alternative.	Same as Alternative C.
Local Economics	Same as existing conditions.	Moderate improvement to local economics with increase in visitors and projects.	Minor improvement to local economics with increase in visitors and projects.	Same as Alternative C.
Environmental Justice	Same as existing conditions.	Moderate benefit to local communities with increased recreational opportunities and improved access.	Minor benefit to local communities with increased recreational opportunities.	Same as Alternative C.
Land Use	Same as existing conditions.	Reduced land use conflicts with improved access control.	Same as Alternative B with greater access control and minor land use change with de-designation of a Research Natural Area.	Same as Alternative C with additional access control.
Aesthetics	Same as existing conditions.	Minor improvement to aesthetics with habitat protection.	Same as Alternative B.	Same as Alternative B.

Table 3. **Moapa Valley National Wildlife Refuge: Summary of Potential Effects of Implementing Alternatives A, B, or C**

Resource	Alternative A	Alternative B	Alternative C (Preferred Alternative)
Physical Environment			
Soils	Temporary adverse effects related to soil erosion during restoration activities.	Same as Alternative A, only slightly more adverse and potential loss of topsoil from facility construction. Best Management Practices (BMPs) would reduce impacts on soil.	Same as Alternative B, only more adverse.
Surface Water Quality	Potential temporary adverse effects on water quality during restoration near springs, streams, and open water sources. Long-term improvement in water quality with restoration of native vegetation.	Same as Alternative A, only slightly more adverse with additional restoration and facility construction. Greater long-term benefit from increased restoration. BMPs would reduce impacts on water quality.	Same as Alternative B, only more adverse. Greater long-term benefit from increased restoration.
Air Quality	Temporary adverse construction emissions during restoration activities. Similar traffic-related emissions as current conditions.	Temporary adverse construction emissions during restoration activities and facility construction (more adverse than Alternative A). Minor long-term increase in traffic-related emissions. Minor temporary adverse impacts from prescribed burns. BMPs would reduce impacts on air quality.	Same as Alternative B, only more adverse.
Biological Resources			
Riparian Habitat	Temporary disturbance with long-term benefit from restoration activities.	Temporary disturbance with long-term benefit from restoration activities and fire management actions. Potential minor loss of vegetation from facility construction. Standard construction measures would reduce impacts during construction.	Same as Alternative B with slightly more disturbance and greater long-term benefit.
Upland Habitat	Same as existing conditions.	Minor loss of vegetation from facility construction. Long-term benefit from invasive plant control and habitat protection efforts. Standard construction measures would reduce impacts during construction.	Same as Alternative B.

Table 3.   Moapa Valley National Wildlife Refuge: Summary of Potential Effects of Implementing Alternatives A, B, or C

Resource	Alternative A	Alternative B	Alternative C (Preferred Alternative)
Biological Resources, continued			
Invasive Plants	Long-term benefit from removal of invasive plants at restoration areas.	Same as Alternative A, only greater benefit.	Same as Alternative B.
Common Wildlife Species	Potential minor temporary adverse impacts from restoration activities. Long-term benefit from habitat restoration.	Same as Alternative A, only more adverse impacts and greater long-term benefits from habitat restoration and protection. Standard construction measures would reduce impacts during construction.	Same as Alternative B with a greater benefit from restoration and Refuge expansion.
Riparian Species	Potential temporary adverse impacts from restoration activities. Minor long-term benefit from riparian habitat restoration.	Greater potential for temporary adverse impacts from increased construction and restoration activities. Greater long-term benefit from riparian habitat restoration. Pre-construction surveys and standard construction measures could reduce impacts during construction and restoration.	Same as Alternative B with a greater long-term benefit from restoration and Refuge expansion.
Desert Tortoise/Gila Monster	Same as existing conditions.	Potential for temporary adverse impacts from construction activities. Long-term benefit from habitat protection. Pre-construction surveys and standard construction measures could reduce impacts during construction.	Same as Alternative B with a greater long-term benefit from Refuge expansion.
Sensitive Fish	Potential temporary adverse impacts from restoration activities. Improved habitat conditions with restoration.	Greater potential for temporary adverse impacts from increased construction and restoration activities. Greater long-term benefit from habitat restoration. Seasonal construction and standard construction measures, including BMPs, could reduce impacts during construction and restoration.	Same as Alternative B with a greater long-term benefit from restoration and Refuge expansion.

Table 3. **Moapa Valley National Wildlife Refuge: Summary of Potential Effects of Implementing Alternatives A, B, or C**

Resource	Alternative A	Alternative B	Alternative C (Preferred Alternative)
Cultural Resources			
Buried Cultural Resources	Potential adverse impacts on buried cultural resources during ground-disturbance activities.	Slightly increased potential adverse impacts on buried cultural resources during ground-disturbance activities. Mitigation measures could reduce impacts to resources during ground-disturbance.	Same as Alternative B, only greater potential with more activities.
Public Access and Recreation			
Public Access	Same as existing conditions.	Improved long-term access with new visitor facilities and opening the Refuge on a limited basis.	Same as Alternative B with opening the Refuge on a daily basis.
Recreation	Same as existing conditions.	Expanded long-term recreation opportunities.	Same as Alternative B with more long-term opportunities.
Social and Economic Conditions			
Refuge Management	Same as existing conditions.	Minor increase in Refuge management budget and staff to implement the alternative.	Moderate increase in Refuge management budget and staff to implement the alternative.
Local Economics	Same as existing conditions.	Minor improvement to local economics with increase in visitors and projects.	Moderate improvement to local economics with increase in visitors and projects.
Environmental Justice	Same as existing conditions.	Minor benefit to local communities with increased recreational opportunities and improved access.	Moderate benefit to local communities with increased recreational opportunities and improved access.
Land Use	Same as existing conditions.	Same as existing conditions.	Improved Refuge management with expansion of Refuge.
Aesthetics	Same as existing conditions.	Minimal adverse impacts from construction and restoration. Long-term benefits from habitat restoration.	Same as Alternative B with a greater long-term benefit.

Table 4. Pahranagat National Wildlife Refuge: Summary of Potential Effects of Implementing Alternatives A, B, C, or D

Resource	Alternative A	Alternative B	Alternative C	Alternative D (Preferred Alternative)
Physical Environment				
Soils	Potential for soil erosion from restoration activities.	Potential for soil erosion from construction and restoration activities. Best Management Practices (BMPs) would reduce impacts on soil.	Same as Alternative B, only greater potential for soil erosion from increased activities.	Same as Alternative C, only greater potential for soil erosion from increased activities.
Surface Water Hydrology	Improved hydrology from restoration activities.	Same as Alternative A.	Same as Alternative A.	Same as Alternative A, only greater improvement with additional restoration.
Surface Water Quality	Temporary impacts to surface water quality from restoration activities.	Temporary impacts to surface water quality from construction and restoration activities. BMPs would reduce impacts on water quality.	Same as Alternative B, only increased impacts from additional activities and herbicide use.	Same as Alternative C.
Water Use	Same as existing conditions.	Modified and expanded water use from increased visitor use and restoration. Mitigation measures could reduce impacts on the groundwater table.	Same as Alternative B.	Same as Alternative B with additional water rights.
Air Quality	Temporary adverse emissions during restoration activities and prescribed burns. Similar traffic-related emissions as existing conditions.	Temporary adverse construction emissions during construction and restoration activities and prescribed burns. Minor long-term increase in traffic-related emissions. BMPs would reduce impacts on air quality.	Same as Alternative B, only slightly more adverse.	Same as Alternative C, only more adverse.
Biological Resources				
Wetland and Open Water Habitat	Temporary disturbance with long-term benefit from restoration.	Same as Alternative A.	Same as Alternative A.	Same as Alternative A with greater long-term benefit with additional restoration.
Riparian Habitat	Temporary disturbance with long-term benefit from restoration.	Same as Alternative A.	Same as Alternative A, only greater benefit over long-term with additional restoration.	Same as Alternative C with greater long-term benefit.

Table 4.   Pahranagat National Wildlife Refuge: Summary of Potential Effects of Implementing Alternatives A, B, C, or D

Resource	Alternative A	Alternative B	Alternative C	Alternative D (Preferred Alternative)
Biological Resources, continued				
Upland Habitat	Same as existing conditions.	Minor loss of vegetation from construction. Long-term benefit from habitat protection. Standard construction measures would reduce impacts during construction.	Same as Alternative B with additional disturbance from construction, but greater benefit from increased protection.	Same as Alternative C with additional protection.
Invasive Plants	Same as existing conditions.	Minor increase in invasive plant removal efforts.	Moderate increase in invasive plant removal efforts.	Same as Alternative C.
Common Wildlife Species	Potential minor temporary adverse impacts from restoration activities. Long-term benefit from restoration.	Potential temporary adverse impacts from restoration and construction activities. Long-term benefits from habitat restoration. Standard construction measures would reduce impacts during construction.	Same as Alternative B, only slightly greater potential for temporary impacts and greater long-term benefit.	Same as Alternative C, only greater potential for temporary impacts and greater long-term benefit.
Desert Tortoise	Same as existing conditions.	Potential temporary adverse impacts from construction activities. Minor long-term benefit from habitat protection. Pre-construction surveys and standard construction measures could reduce impacts during construction.	Same as Alternative B, only slightly greater potential for construction impacts and greater long-term benefit from increased protection.	Same as Alternative C with additional protection.
Migratory Birds	Potential temporary adverse impacts from restoration activities. Long-term benefit from restoration.	Same as Alternative A. Pre-construction surveys and standard construction measures could reduce impacts during construction.	Same as Alternative A, only greater benefit over the long term with additional restoration.	Same as Alternative C with greater long-term benefit.
Pahranagat Roundtail Chub	Same as existing conditions.	Long-term benefit from refugium construction.	Same as Alternative A.	Same as Alternative A.

Table 4.   Pahranagat National Wildlife Refuge: Summary of Potential Effects of Implementing Alternatives A, B, C, or D

Resource	Alternative A	Alternative B	Alternative C	Alternative D (Preferred Alternative)
Cultural Resources				
Buried Cultural Resources	Same as existing conditions.	Potential adverse impacts on buried cultural resources during ground-disturbance activities. Mitigation measures could reduce impacts to resources during ground disturbance.	Same as Alternative B with slightly greater potential due to increased ground disturbance.	Same as Alternative C with greater potential due to increased ground disturbance.
Aboveground Cultural Resources	Same as existing conditions (vandalism and degradation with minimal protection efforts).	Reduced potential for vandalism or degradation of cultural resources from visitor use from increased protection efforts.	Same as Alternative B, only less potential with increased protection.	Same as Alternative C, only less potential with increased protection.
Public Access and Recreation				
Public Access	Same as existing conditions.	Temporary access restrictions during construction activities. Improved long-term access with facility improvements. Mitigation measures would reduce access restrictions during construction.	Same as Alternative B with greater temporary access restrictions.	Same as Alternative C with increased control of access.
Recreation	Same as existing conditions.	Temporary restrictions on activities during construction activities. Improved and expanded long-term recreation opportunities.	Same as Alternative B with greater temporary activity restrictions and more long-term opportunities.	Same as Alternative C.
Social and Economic Conditions				
Refuge Management	Same as existing conditions.	Minor increase in Refuge management budget and staff to implement the alternative.	Moderate increase in Refuge management budget and staff to implement the alternative.	Same as Alternative C.
Local Economics	Same as existing conditions.	Minor improvement to local economics with increase in visitors and projects.	Moderate improvement to local economics with increase in visitors and projects.	Same as Alternative C.
Environmental Justice	Same as existing conditions.	Minor benefit to local communities with increased recreational opportunities and improved access.	Moderate benefit to local communities with increased recreational opportunities and improved access.	Same as Alternative C.

Table 4. Pahranagat National Wildlife Refuge: Summary of Potential Effects of Implementing Alternatives A, B, C, or D

Resource	Alternative A	Alternative B	Alternative C	Alternative D (Preferred Alternative)
Social and Economic Conditions, continued				
Aesthetics	Minor improvement to aesthetics with habitat restoration.	Temporary adverse impacts on aesthetics during construction activities. Long-term benefit from restoration activities. Mitigation measures could reduce construction impacts.	Same as Alternative B, only greater impacts with more activities.	Same as Alternative C.